BEYOND
KNOWING

BEYOND KNOWING

MYSTERIES AND MESSAGES OF DEATH AND LIFE FROM A FORENSIC PATHOLOGIST

JANIS AMATUZIO, MD

NEW WORLD LIBRARY
NOVATO, CALIFORNIA

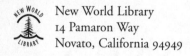 New World Library
14 Pamaron Way
Novato, California 94949

Text design and typography by Tona Pearce Myers

ISBN-13: 978-1-57731-550-6

Printed in the U.S.A.

g A proud member of the Green Press Initiative

Distributed by Publishers Group West

For Calvin Bandt, MD,
1933–2003,
extraordinary physician and forensic pathologist
and my beloved friend and mentor,
who taught me more than I could ever imagine.
Also for
all who trust life,
gracing their days with kindness, courage, and compassion.

CONTENTS

Part IV. The Third Secret: We Are Awakening

Part V. The Fourth Secret: We Are All Connected

Part VI. The Fifth Secret: There Is No Need to Fear

Part VII. The Sixth Secret: All Is Well

PREFACE

As a forensic pathologist for more than twenty-five years, I have the extraordinary privilege of speaking for the dead by investigating their circumstances of death. This means examining the body and clothing; learning about personal habits, intimate beliefs, and customs; and safeguarding valuables, photographs, and other treasured possessions. I use my medical knowledge and life experience to interpret and diagnose patterns of disease, disuse, and injury. My goal is always to reveal the truth about "what happened," so loved ones can mourn, understand, and return to life wiser than before.

Occasionally loved ones speak of extraordinary experiences: dreams, visions, or synchronicities surrounding the event of a death that have deeply affected their lives. These mysteries have long fascinated me and led me to write my first book, *Forever Ours*.

In *Forever Ours*, my heart still harbored some uncertainty, and my thoughts were centered on the hope implicit in the *what if* of the question "What if these extraordinary experiences are true?" Additionally, I knew that as a scientist and physician, I could not "prove" these experiences to any "reasonable" degree of medical certainty. And I was concerned that my interest would draw ridicule and criticism from my colleagues and associates. However, quite the contrary has happened; my community has supported me. Physicians and nurses, law enforcement and emergency personnel, county commissioners, and family members have applauded and encouraged the recounting of these experiences.

Their support has given me the courage to pursue my observations, and to look more deeply at the dreams, visions, and extraordinary experiences that so many people report following the death of a loved one. As a result, my second book was written from a slightly different perspective and is accompanied by a deep sense of calm. It was created to help me live more meaningfully *with* these experiences. It was written so I could glean the knowledge inherent in these experiences and apply it to my own life.

As I have studied those who have shared an experience with me, I have observed that they are profoundly changed and live life differently than they did before, with an inner knowing that seems to create health and beauty wherever they go. These observations are the subject of this book.

In *Beyond Knowing* I explore the wisdom and truths arising from these mysteriously beautiful experiences: an awareness that we already know these things; insights that trigger freedom and joy; and the recognition of profound loving reassurance that life is perfectly safe and always goes on. For me, these beautiful secrets are the wisdom that reshapes the deepest foundations of our thoughts and causes the creation of a fuller, grander, and more meaningful experience of life.

What had changed in the intervening years between my two books?

Of course, the answer is, I did. I guess it could best be described as a shift in my own awareness, from a sense of hope to one of knowing — that we *are* immortal and forever is a long, long time — a shift marked by feelings of excitement and purpose as well as profound happiness. You see, as a physician, I realize the importance of "being healthy" and of "leading by example." I also know that we teach that which we need most to learn or remember.

But please don't take my experience as recorded in this book as "the truth." Read the words on these pages and the stories that real people have shared with me. Then trust your own feelings, make your own decisions, arrive at your own truth, about one of the greatest concerns of sentient humanity: Life and Death.

When I was a student at the University of Minnesota Medical School, I did what all physicians in training before me had done. I studied anatomy and physiology, immunology and biochemistry; I sought and memorized patterns of health and disease; and I rediscovered the science and art that are the foundation of medicine. A saying I remember well from that time runs: "Study hard and learn well. The dead have much to teach the living." Perhaps now is the time for us to look at the immortal mysteries that those who have died can truly teach the living.

INTRODUCTION

It would have been easy to dismiss them, these experiences that have no name, that usually start with phrases like "You won't believe this..." or "Doctor, there is something else..." — but I couldn't. When I spoke with family members following the investigation into the death of a loved one, occasionally I would hear of an extraordinary coincidence, dream, or experience. I would listen, and frequently I would write down what they told me. At first I viewed these incidents as just another "unusual" forensic finding. However, as time went on, something changed. Something inside me awakened, and I felt as though I'd caught a glimpse of something grand I had not expected. I felt jolted back to remembering but remembering what? Something very familiar. Let me explain.

Although most autopsies performed at our office are part

of a death investigation for one of the forensic systems we serve, occasionally a nonforensic case is referred for other reasons, for example, to explain a disease process or to complete hospital tests. Recently, a woman named Laura requested an autopsy to help her family understand what had really happened to her husband following organ transplant surgery. The hospital course was long and difficult, and his last few weeks were a desperate and losing struggle. The ravages of the disease had taken their toll on his body and his ability to heal. After I performed the autopsy and reviewed the medical records, I scheduled a meeting with the family to review my findings. During that meeting, the extent of their concern and frustration was evident.

I answered Laura's questions as well as I could. We discussed the devastating effects of his disease and its complications and the complexities of organ transplants. She seemed satisfied, though still visibly sad. As she was leaving, Laura thanked me and told me she appreciated my time and efforts. "I miss him terribly," she said, "but this has really helped us. I know now we did everything we could." Her daughter nodded and looked down. Laura reached out to shake my extended hand and hesitated. "Doctor, could I tell you something else?"

"Of course you can," I said, sitting back down at the conference table.

"Something happened to me last evening," she said, taking a deep breath. "I had been on the road for several hours, driving up to my daughter's house to stay overnight for this meeting. I was thinking about my husband, Ron, our children, and our life together. As the memories flooded over me,

I felt such overwhelming grief that I burst into tears and just wept. I knew I had to pay attention to my driving, so I took a deep breath and wiped my eyes and rolled down the window. I punched on the radio to break the silence and distract my thoughts, but what happened next absolutely astonished me!

"The radio came on quite loud; instantly I recognized the music that filled my car — it was 'our song,' from 1981. Ron liked it so well he had given it to me on an eight-track tape. I listened to the familiar verses playing on the radio, and the words 'being well in heaven' and 'watching over you' took on a whole new meaning. I was just plainly amazed. It reminded me of one of the best times in our life together.

"In that moment I changed; I mean, I *knew* without a doubt he was reaching out to assure me that all was well.

"When I pulled into my daughter's driveway, I turned off the engine and spent a few moments in silence, memories flooding over me. What an astonishing coincidence, Doctor! I think he knew, somehow, that I was thinking of him . . . and he wanted to let me know. I felt like we were dancing together again!"

She smiled warmly, paused, and with a deep, slow sigh added, "I'll be okay now. Thank you." And she turned to go.

With a sense of wonder, I watched her walk down the hall with her daughter. Over the years of practicing forensic pathology, I have heard a number of these experiences, but each time I am filled with wonder.

As I began to collect and study these mysterious and extraordinary experiences, I could not help but notice their amazing and profound effects: palpable joy, relief and reassurance, comfort and calm, hearts seeming healed. I began asking those who shared an experience, "How has this changed your life?"

The answers were astonishingly similar in their elegant simplicity and beauty: It's all about love. All is well. Be kind. Trust yourself. Don't worry. Live each day to the fullest. Life is a phenomenal gift. There is nothing to fear. Everything is *really* all right.

I also began to realize that masters and prophets through-out the centuries have shared such words, and I was struck with a sense of awe. Perhaps these experiences are immortal gifts, age-old portals through which we can reach into the realm of the masters and mystics, approach the threshold of the divine, and glean the wisdom of the ages. Could the magic and power in these familiar stories transform us as they have others?

In a time when many sense an urgency to seek new answers to age-old questions and to temper beliefs and behaviors that lead to violence, our interest in these extraordinary experiences seems no coincidence.

It has been said that peace in the world begins with peace in the hearts of the people. Perhaps the patterns of wisdom inherent in these experiences could ignite the grandest hopes of man-*kind*. Perhaps through the retelling of these experiences, we may reshape our thoughts, act differently, and remember all over again who we *really* are — and in the process remember how to create heaven on earth. What an extraordinary thought . . . what an extraordinary hope.

IT IS SAID THAT WITH PRACTICE comes knowledge and with experience comes wisdom.

As I have listened to the extraordinary experiences told to me by family members and loved ones of those whose deaths I have investigated, I have come to see more than I expected. I have begun to "know" something special is unfolding all around me. Maybe it's just what happens with study and practice — or perhaps it has been a grand coincidence. But after hearing and recording a number of these extraordinary experiences, one day I began to see unexpectedly beautiful patterns of truth in the messages of the visions, dreams, and synchronicities.

What is a pattern? Something you recognize, a familiar path, a common thread, a constellation of stars in the night sky creating a picture that points the way, that helps you to remember, to orient yourself. Most important, perhaps, a pattern is something you recognize that is *true for you*.

Hope, compassion, and wisdom emerged from the space around these experiences. And quite unexpectedly, extraordinary joy and peace began to touch my heart.

Perhaps this is what I intended all along.

PART I

THE UNFOLDING

I believe that imagination is stronger than knowledge —
That myth is more potent than history.
That dreams are more powerful than facts —
That hope always triumphs over experience —
That laughter is the only cure for grief.
And I believe that love is stronger than death.

— ROBERT FULGHUM, "STORYTELLER'S CREED,"
IT WAS ON FIRE WHEN I LAY DOWN ON IT

DREAM DAYS

Imagination is more important than knowledge.

— ALBERT EINSTEIN

H ow did you get this way?" an old friend recently asked me over lunch.

"What way?" I answered.

"You know, the way you are..."

"You mean a forensic pathologist with a book? No, I know what you mean," I answered with a grin. "I'm just being Janis."

"Just Janis" has been a joke in our family ever since I was very young, five or six, I think, and was learning how to answer the phone. A family friend called to speak with my mother. Apparently surprised that I had answered, she asked, "Who is this?"

"Oh, just Janis," I replied, startled, and I abruptly dropped the phone and ran for my mother.

But I think if I answer my friend's question, and explain how "just Janis" got this way, that might make this collection of stories and experiences more meaningful for the reader.

WHEN I WAS A LITTLE GIRL, my mother always said I had a vivid imagination; but then again, I had an extraordinary family. When I was young, I had not one but two imaginary friends who used to play with me for hours around the house. Their names were Rara and Gerry, and they were always there whenever I wanted to play. With them, I made up new games, fairy castles, and magic places. And then there were my animals, especially Morgi, my well-worn, soft stuffed dog with blue button eyes, a big black nose, and the red tongue that my "Gammy" (my mother's mother) sewed back on at least a dozen times.

During the Korean War, my father served in the Naval Medical Corps, which supplied the physicians for the Marine Corps. My dad was stationed at a Marine base in Japan, treating the sick and wounded. I don't remember seeing him leave, except I noticed that my Gammy came to stay with Mother and me. I was thrilled to have such a wonderful companion who would take me for walks, read to me always, and play for hours in the sandbox. Those were very good days. Later, my younger brother, Barry, and sister, Patty, were added to the family — as well as the dachshunds Fritzie and Piccolo.

I grew up watching my mother and father work very hard. From them I learned to set goals and set them high. My mother would say you could accomplish anything if you set your mind to it. So I did. I graduated at the top of my high school class, won a young artists piano competition and performed at Northrop Auditorium at the University of Minnesota, became a ski instructor and a water safety instructor, and graduated from medical school and residency training with all the associated examinations. I really can work — I really have worked — *very* hard!

But there is another part to me, as well, a part that doesn't really believe in working quite so hard, even though work seems to be a habit I learned very well. That part of me loves to just play and dance and read; that is the largely unexplored part of my adult self, one I still at times have to give myself permission to be.

So, how did I get what my friend called "this way"? I have begun to pay more attention to the part of me that doesn't need to work hard, and I have remembered that the "extraordinary" seems to *be there* whenever I take time to be "just Janis" — to stop, to listen to a patient or a family member, to laugh or joke with them, or for myself to just sleep, play, or reflect.

This awareness seems to have everything to do with what I am *not* doing. Now, when I pause, I see threads of magical awareness woven into the fabric of my life from the beginning. Most of the time as they were happening, I only caught a glimpse. As I have begun to realize they are there, I have become gently aware of the extraordinary love that surrounds me. Always.

I VIVIDLY REMEMBER THE DAY Dad finally came home from Korea. I was almost three years old, and he looked so happy and so handsome that Mother tells me I had a sudden attack of shyness and hid behind the counter. But Dad must have anticipated my reticence — tucked under his arm was a big, white, fluffy dog with a pink ribbon around her neck, and as soon as I noticed the dog, my shyness disappeared.

I was delighted as he gently put the dog, already named

Fee-Fee, in my arms. I listened with wide eyes as he told me how Fee-Fee helped drive the airplane that brought him home from the hospital in Japan. The flight had been rough, and Fee-Fee had braved storms and winds and all sorts of hardships to make sure everyone was safe. Dad said she even wore goggles and a helmet but he had had to leave those behind for the other pilots. I knew that doggie was a hero like my Dad and treated her accordingly.

Fee-Fee became my best friend and constant companion; she even slept under the covers with me every night and guarded the edge of the bed. She gradually lost her bow, her fur, and her stuffing. One day, many years later, she mysteriously disappeared. I still wonder what happened.

I know my mother was right about my imagination. But I also know that my father had one too, and he tantalized us with his incredible stories, dreams, and wild tales of adventure. When Mother would nod in agreement, I just knew the stories had to be true! Now I reflect back on long ago and have to laugh at myself, since my imaginary friends, as well as Fee-Fee and Morgi, seem as real to me today as they did then.

However, as an adult and author, occasionally I, too, wonder about my "vivid imagination" in relationship to all the extraordinary synchronicities and experiences I have recorded. Not long ago, a physician colleague laughingly asked me, "Do you think you have been making it all up?" His comment caught me up short when he said it, and I vigorously denied any suggestion of the sort. But later, when I was alone, I painfully pondered his suggestion.

THEN I REMEMBERED SOMETHING FORGOTTEN, one of my earliest memories — an experience marked by a feeling of what I can only describe as ecstasy. I realize now, as I write these words, the memory is still marked by that bliss. Let me set the stage.

My mother, Verda Ann Barry, came from humble beginnings, growing up in Sisseton, South Dakota. She was the youngest of four children born to Margaret Bridget O'Brien and Clyde Burton Barry. Her father was a day laborer, and her mother tended to the family and made extra money cooking for threshing crews in the fall and later keeping the books at a local dry goods store. My mother grew up in a home most would consider poor. Hard work, home cooking, homemade clothes, honest living, and the love of her family surrounded her.

Her parents encouraged her to go on to school after she graduated at the top of her high school class as valedictorian. They were thrilled when she was accepted into the nurses training program at Eitel Hospital in Minneapolis, for she was the first in her family to receive any education past high school. Mother, too, was proud and excited. However, when she boarded the train to leave Sisseton for the Twin Cities the first time, she told me, she cried all the way there.

During her nurses training she met my father, Donald Amatuzio, then a senior medical student. He had grown up in West Duluth, Minnesota, the oldest of five children born to Margaret Chiovotti and Alberto Blaze Amatuzio, who had both emigrated from Italy with their families in the early 1900s. My father was the first in his family to attend college. He began his studies at the University of Minnesota in the school of engineering, but in the middle of his second year, he applied to medical school on a dare from a classmate. He was accepted into medical school for the fall — a decision that changed the course of his life.

My parents were married during World War II, after Mother graduated from nurses' training and Dad from medical school. My father had an internship at Mercy Hospital in Chicago and then did a tour of duty in the navy. After the war he pursued residency training in internal medicine and chest and heart disease. My mother practiced nursing for six years, until I was born and my father was called back into service for the Korean conflict.

Since Mother stayed home with her children, we three blissfully felt we had her undivided attention. Her quiet and gentle energy permeated everything she did, from painting beautiful ceramics to knitting to cooking and cleaning. I began helping her clean the house very early on; she would run the vacuum, and I would carry the cord! She insisted on order in our home, which led to familiar routines that I recognize in myself to this day. One of them was eating dinner all together every evening at six o'clock sharp; another was my practicing the piano for an hour every morning before school. And more important, we were all in bed every night on schedule, although on Sunday nights it was after *Lassie* and *Disneyland*, and in later years, after watching Hoss and Little Joe on *Bonanza*.

Before I started school at age four, I had an afternoon nap right after lunch. Mother would firmly insist on the nap, even when I protested that I wasn't tired at all. She would humor me sometimes by letting me sleep on her and my father's bed, which was covered with a white cotton bedspread with fringe on the edges. (I always hoped this privilege was granted only to me as the oldest child!)

I remember one particular afternoon when Mother let me nap on the big bed. She pulled down the window shades, covered me with a light blanket, and kissed me on the cheek. She shut the bedroom door behind her, and I drifted off to sleep. What happened next I recall as if it were yesterday. A large, light-filled being appeared at my bedside. He was surrounded by soft white light laced with brilliant dancing colors as if they were bouncing from a prism in bright sunlight. He was so familiar in such an intimate way, it was as if I had known him forever. He took my hand gently and lifted me effortlessly up out of bed.

The light surrounded both of us yet didn't hurt my eyes. It was warm and comforting. I began to play with it, and colors bounced and swirled with just the touch of my hand. I remember splashing and swirling them, and laughing with joy when they began to take on form. Then he took my hand, and together we left the bedroom. The beautiful light continued to swirl around us, and suddenly two luminous horses emerged to carry us high above the earth. We soared over the most beautiful land ever seen, filled with all the colors of the rainbow and more. The hues in the light seemed to shimmer and vibrate as if alive, connecting heaven and earth.

As we soared on the backs of the beautiful horses, the being told me he was my guardian and guide. Without words, with only his thoughts, he told me he would accompany me throughout my entire life, as if riding by my side. He sent a wave of light streaming toward me. I remember reaching for it and wrapping it around me. As I did, an amazing feeling of love, joy, and ecstasy filled my heart, as well as a knowing . . . that together we would grace the land with beautiful light. I knew that I had never been so happy as right then and there.

I AM NOT SURE whether that magical afternoon was the beginning of my awakening or perhaps the end of my childhood "remembering," since I don't recall anything remotely similar happening until many years later.

Now as I reflect again on my colleague's comment, I smile to myself, as I realize I have felt a lifelong connection with horses (Eddie, Mo, Cee, Charlie, and Rudy, to mention a few), who have graced my life and given me great happiness. I also have begun to recognize the gentle and reassuring presence of my "guide"; those moments are always marked by deep reassurance and joy.

MEDICAL SCHOOL DAZE

I was accepted into medical school at the University of Minnesota in the fall of 1973. There were almost two hundred students in the freshman class, and twelve of us were women. I was excited, proud, and scared all at the same time on the first days of class. High energy was in the air as we were introduced to our instructors, given our ID cards and name tags, and assigned to our classroom and shiny blue lockers. The freshman class of '73 was the first group to have classes in the new med school building. The bright colors, fresh paint, and clean floors of Building A seemed to reflect our enthusiasm and fervor.

We studied many fascinating and not-so-fascinating subjects that first year, but by far the class that both terrified and excited me most was human anatomy. It was offered in one of the old buildings, Jackson Hall — in the same room, in fact, where my father had taken the class so many years before. There we were privileged to learn by actually examining and dissecting a real arterially embalmed human body. Four medical students were assigned to each table.

The huge human anatomy laboratory room was on the third floor, in the northwest corner of Jackson Hall. Large oak trees lined busy Washington Avenue below, and that fall, their gold and red leaves filled the windows with vivid color.

My first and strongest impression of the class was the overwhelmingly pungent odor. The smell of formaldehyde and embalming fluid literally permeated the walls and clung to the floors and ceilings. Three other medical students and I were assigned to our cadaver station, which was, fortunately, located in the corner of the room and was flanked by big windows on each side. We routinely opened them wide to ease the smell, but nothing could erase it from our memory.

All the bodies we examined were generous gifts or donations, bequeathed by families or at the request of the person before death. That knowledge did not really reduce my apprehension about what I would see, and I let the three other students at our table elevate the body from its stainless steel storage container to table-top height and unzip the bag. I must admit, I was surprised at my reaction. As the body bag was slowly opened, I wasn't frightened or upset, but was quite relieved. Our cadaver was a petite, pretty, elderly woman with pale blonde-gray hair, fair skin, and neatly painted rose-colored fingernails. She wasn't scary at all; actually, she looked like the wife of one of my father's medical school friends, Edith, and that promptly became her name! My three male medical student partners were slightly amused, but they agreed that the name fit. Edith and I spent from twelve to twenty hours together each week in the anatomy lab that first year, as I carefully dissected and identified the veins, arteries, and nerves in her arms and legs, neck, chest, abdomen, and head, learned the relationships of the organs to one another, and always, always memorized my newfound knowledge each step of the way.

Curiously, one early October afternoon stands out in my mind. We had been in school for almost a month and a half by then, enough time to begin to grapple with the heavy workload and to realize there was no time in the day for anything except attending class, studying, eating, and sleeping. In fact, I really didn't have time to think about myself at all, only about studying and passing exams.

That particular afternoon our dissection centered on the upper arm, and my partner, Paul, and I, were laboriously dissecting the vessels, muscles, and nerves of the right arm. The windows were wide open, and a warm, sweet wind gently blew gusts of fresh air into our corner. I looked up suddenly and glanced outside. For some reason my glance landed on a gray squirrel staring intently at me from his safe perch on a limb not far from the window. In that moment it was as though my point of view suddenly shifted, as if I were outside myself looking into the cadaver laboratory.

I became acutely aware of the warmth of the autumn sunlight, the rustle of the leaves in the gusts of wind, the constant stream of traffic below, and the rugged feel of the bark of the tree. It seemed that time ceased in that moment, and my aware-ness telescoped a thousand times. A perception of great beauty and familiar stillness filled my heart; I was both startled and delighted at the sudden shift. I knew in that instant, somehow, all was well and had been perfectly created for just that time and space. All of it was exquisitely interlinked. I wondered why I had never noticed things that way before.

The experience passed quickly, and I was back again. My attention refocused on the anatomy lab, my studies, and the work in front of me. However, a pervasive sense of peacefulness filled my heart, one that had not been there moments before. The shift had occurred spontaneously, and the moment passed, almost without my noticing.

Time flew by quickly in all my busyness; weeks became months, which melted rapidly into years. Constant study be-came a habit, and I began to look forward to applying my new-found knowledge.

The last two years of medical school were filled with rota-tions of a month to six weeks in different subspecialties, such as ophthalmology, surgery, ear, nose, and throat, or ENT, and emergency medicine. We had the chance to choose the areas we were interested in, although some, like pediatrics, surgery, and neurology, were required. We also quickly recognized which rotations and instructors were difficult and demanding and which ones were a whole lot easier.

In the spring of my fourth year in medical school, I had just finished two grueling rotations, one in oncology, the care of cancer patients, and the other in internal medicine, the general care of adults. I had selected these areas for study since I hoped to follow my father into internal medicine, possibly one day joining him in practice.

I remember feeling weary that fall from the intense pace, and I decided to choose an easier assignment for my next rotation in order to begin studying for part 2 of the National Board Examination. Given the many hours we had to put in, little things like sleeping rooms, hot showers, and meals became very important. Rumor had it that the GI medicine rotation — gastrointestinal, the study of diseases of the stomach and intestines — at the Veterans Administration (VA) Hospital was a "walk in the park," and better yet, the food was supposed to be superb! I decided to select it for my next clinical rotation.

My dad was always keenly interested in my medical education, and being a voracious reader and perpetual student himself, he would frequently quiz me on medical facts (ones I desperately hoped I knew!). Over Christmas dinner that year, Dad casually asked about my choices for clinical rotations for the upcoming semester. I told him my thoughts, between mouthfuls of Christmas lasagna, about GI medicine at the VA Hospital and the great free meals at the hospital cafeteria. I'll never forget his response. He slowly put down his fork, leaned forward, and cleared his throat.

"Janis, you will take pathology from Dr. Bob Anderson at Hennepin County Medical Center, and your mother will make your sandwiches!"

"But, Dad!" I pleaded, "GI medicine is supposed to be real good at the VA..."

"Pathology is the basis of medicine, Janis, and Dr. Robert Anderson is the finest man I know in the field. He'll take good care of you. Subject closed!"

The subject was truly closed, and I reluctantly reassigned myself to the six-week pathology rotation at the Hennepin County Medical Center that year. Little did I know then that the course of my life was about to change dramatically.

NINE BODY BAGS

Autopsy: to see with one's own eyes.

In 1976, the pathology department office was located in the basement of the newly built Hennepin County Medical Center. By now I have come to realize that most pathology offices are located in the basement. I don't view this, however, as a metaphor for what my father called "the basis of medicine"; rather, the offices are usually just placed close to the morgue and autopsy suites, which are almost always in the cool, windowless basements.

The lower-level hospital hallways had a complex overhead rail system that transported large, color-coded plastic lockers filled with laundry, supplies, and surgical scrubs between the hospital and the adjacent laundry building. We quickly learned to duck and dive around and between them as we made our way to the laboratory upstairs or the morgue down the hall.

The pathology office and the hospital shared the coolers and autopsy suite with the office of the Hennepin County medical examiner, which was located in the northeast corner of the hospital complex. The medical students on the pathology service were required to assist with and perform several autopsies on hospital patients and correlate their diseases with the medical history and hospital course.

I remember well the first autopsy I performed; it was on an elderly man who had died of pneumonia. My clinical training in physical diagnosis and medical school anatomy and physiology seemed to come together in an amazing way. In what can only be described as an "Oh my!!" experience, it all began to make sense. The right lower lobe of his lung was consolidated by the infection and covered with cloudy yellow-gray fluid. My excitement grew as I visualized diseases and understood their diagnoses; I realized the value of "seeing with my own eyes."

In the autopsy suite, we worked side by side with the staff forensic pathologists and the forensic pathology resident-in-training or forensic fellow. Frequently I would observe them working with law enforcement officers on a difficult postmortem examination. I might catch a glimpse of a gunshot or a stab wound or perhaps a ruptured cerebral aneurysm, which had caused an unexpected death. Mostly, I observed from a distance, since I was keenly aware of the legal consequences of forensic findings.

But one day was different. Dr. Kenny Osterberg, the Hennepin County assistant medical examiner, had been asked to examine the remains of an unknown number of people who had perished in a hotel fire in a small rural town. The medical examiner's office accepted referral cases from smaller counties whenever specialized forensic services were required. This was such a case. The hotel had burned to the ground during the night. The local coroner was overwhelmed and asked for help, not only with the determination of the cause of death but also with identification of the victims. Since the forensic fellow was already busy with a different case, I was lucky enough to be asked to assist Dr. Osterberg with this one.

THAT MORNING when the walk-in cooler doors swung wide open, the chilled air sent a shiver down my spine. The odor of smoke and charred remains penetrated even the icy air of the cooler. Bodies were lying on carts and were covered with sheets except for their feet. A toe tag identified each one with the medical examiner's number and a name. A few unidentified bodies simply said JOHN DOE. In the corner on the floor were nine black, heavy-duty body bags, each tightly zipped. As the fourth-year medical student assigned to the autopsy service, I had been asked to help the prosector, or autopsy assistant, set up for this unusual medical examiner's case.

There is a misconception that the job of the forensic pathologist is to perform autopsies only on suspicious or unusual cases. The autopsy or postmortem examination is just one tool that is used to answer the question "What happened?"

Whenever there is a suspicious death, the body should be examined at the death scene, preferably by the forensic pathologist who will be performing the examination. The scene has to be thoroughly investigated both from the perspective of law enforcement crime scene specialists and from the perspective of the forensic pathologist and medical examiner's or coroner's investigator. Both departments must view the scene and together search for clues and telltale evidence. The position of the body, the clothing, and the presence of drugs, needles, or empty pill bottles can reveal the truth about that person's thoughts, habits, and lifestyle, and even about his or her last moments. Viewing the body at the scene of a suspicious death gives the pathologist a unique advantage; she is able to identify the questions that must be answered at the autopsy. She is also able to speak more clearly for the person who has died.

During the scene inspection, investigators also try to confirm the identity of the deceased — technically, make a "positive identification" — so that the next of kin can be notified; information about the deceased's habits, medical history, and recent circumstances can be documented; and personal property can be secured. Occasionally the identity is unknown, and then the forensic specialists resort to other methods, such as comparison of pre- and postmortem dental X-rays, radiographs, descriptions of tattoos, jewelry, or clothing. Now the search can include accessing national databanks of missing persons and using DNA testing when other methods aren't successful.

WHEN THE HOTEL BURNED TO THE GROUND, the number of occupants was unknown, and also the manner in which the fire had started. The scene investigators had been instructed to sift through the rubble and to identify the locations of the bodies. Although the bodies were all badly charred and unrecognizable, the scene investigators tried to place the parts of only one body in each body bag.

The prosector and I carefully placed each sealed black body bag on an autopsy cart, weighed it, and wheeled it into the special autopsy room were Dr. Osterberg and I would be working. The room was small, with just enough room for two autopsy carts, so some of the body bags were respectfully placed on the floor. This method worked well, since many of the remains were both small (due to the effect of heat) and fragmented. Dr. Osterberg had brought a large whiteboard into the room and taped a grid to its surface to help document and organize our data on the remains, any new information, and pending identifications. Although I didn't realize it at the time, he was teaching me the fundamentals of handling a mass disaster. His methods and meticulous attention to detail formed the basis for my future plans and practices.

As investigators from the medical examiner's office and law enforcement agencies sought to gather information about the possible occupants of the hotel, we began the daunting task of examining the remains. After each bag was weighed, it was x-rayed and designated with a number. We then opened the bags to view and photograph the remains. Extensive burning had reduced the bodies to blackened, charred pieces of tissue, unrecognizable as human beings. In most cases only the torso remained. The X-rays proved extremely valuable for identifying and separating the bones from fragments of melted metallic and other debris: nails, wire, and wood from the collapsed building Mostly, we were searching for bullets, since many times someone will attempt to cover up homicidal violence by setting a fire.

We opened the bags methodically and examined the remains carefully. Sometimes we were lucky and discovered a fragment of a jaw, a tooth, or a distinctive bone fragment. Meanwhile, medical records, dental X-rays, and fingerprints began to arrive in the office. The slow and sometimes painstaking process of searching for clues and matching up the remains with the retrieved information took well over two weeks. We identified the bodies one by one, several on the basis of dental records and one on the basis of a metal prosthesis in a hip.

The examinations were fascinating to me, but one in particular I will never forget. I remember leaning over Dr. Osterberg's shoulder as he unzipped the fourth black bag. I had begun to know what to expect, but what I saw next was unbelievable. Bones with freshly sawed ends were protruding from the charred remains; we both stared in shocked surprise. That observation changed absolutely everything. No longer were we fairly certain these were victims of a fire; we began to think they were victims of a homicide.

We examined the rest but found no other sawed bones. Then Dr. Osterberg suggested we examine the sawed bones more carefully by removing the charred flesh. As we gently removed the tissue it became apparent the bones were not human, so Dr. Osterberg called in a consultant from the university veterinary hospital. A day later she called to inform us the bones were those of a large pig; they had evidently been recovered from the kitchen area of the burned building.

And so the story began to unfold. The hotel kitchen was no longer actively serving meals, and although the exact sequence of events would never be known, it appeared the hotel guests had decided to use the kitchen for a pig roast. Evidently the cooking process had been left unattended; the fire had started in the kitchen and engulfed the hotel, first in smoke and then in flames. All of the victims (except for the pig) died from inhalation of smoke and carbon monoxide.

NINE BODY BAGS, eight people, and one pig. I was fascinated by the process of solving the mystery through the application of medicine, forensic pathology, anthropology, dentistry, veterinary medicine, the investigative strategies of law enforcement and the fire marshal — and common sense. I was mesmerized by the mysteries of forensic pathology and certain this could be my future career path.

However, I was also already scheduled to start a highly prized internal medicine internship and residency at the University of Minnesota Hospitals in three months. Dr. Osterberg sat and listened patiently as I explained my dilemma. "Forensic pathology isn't always this exciting, Janis. There are some very difficult cases, and some very difficult days ahead if you choose this specialty. You have always wanted to treat the living, and we deal only with the dead. Why don't you go ahead and do your internship in internal medicine; it's required for a pathology residency anyway. Then you can decide. You know, you would have to take four years of pathology training before you could take a fellowship year in forensic pathology."

I nodded and carefully weighed his words. Later that year, 1977, I graduated from medical school and started the whirlwind of my internal medicine internship three months early, taking the place of a resident who had dropped out. I kept Dr. Osterberg's words of advice tucked safely in the back of my mind, there to review if I ever needed them.

THE HARDEST DAYS
OF MY LIFE: INTERNSHIP

The days of my internal medicine internship at the University of Minnesota Hospitals blurred into weeks, and the weeks into months. I never worked so hard for so long or learned so much. Quickly I became proficient at critical care medicine, fighting off death and managing disease as well as I knew how. The days were grueling. I imagined myself becoming like a warrior: tough, efficient, and capable. I wore my white coat and stethoscope like a badge of honor and prided myself for getting by on three to five hours of sleep each night. I crossed off each day of that year on a wall calendar; I had four off-duty days in twelve months.

There were two care teams on ward 6B, the red team and the blue, each made up of an intern, a second-year resident, and an attending physician. The teams were friendly with each other but also a little competitive. One late-winter afternoon as the nurses changed shifts, I overheard them talking about an unusually difficult patient on the other team — unusual because he was a physician, actually an intern from another program, and difficult because he had aplastic anemia, a condition in which the bone marrow stops producing the essential life-sustaining cells of the blood stream: red cells, white cells, and platelets. This disease was uncommon, usually seen in patients who have had long-term treatment for leukemia.

The patient, Dr. Jeff Hanson, had graduated at the top of his medical school class and was selected to start a residency position in internal medicine at the prestigious Mayo Clinic in Rochester, Minnesota. Unlike most first-year residents, he had taken a few weeks off between medical school and internship, deciding to work on building a log cabin, a dream he had put off for many years. He worked mostly alone, felling the timbers on a beautiful lake property that had long been in his family. After carefully choosing each log, he stripped the bark, shaped the timber, and treated the wood with sealer. He had built the foundation and framed the cabin with the handcrafted logs before he had to return to medicine.

He noticed bruising on his skin several weeks after returning to work and attributed it to bumping into a cart during morning rounds. When the bruises didn't go away, and others appeared, he ran his own blood tests and suspected the diagnosis. The red cell, white cell, and platelet counts in his bloodstream were danger-ously low: his bone marrow wasn't working. After some moments of panic and painful reflection, he thought he knew why. Shortly after treating the logs for his cabin with the chemical sealer, he would pick them up and hoist them into place. Although he wore gloves while he worked, his forearms and tee shirt were frequently soaked with both his sweat and the wood sealer.

The chemical in the sealer, known for its toxicity, was presumed to have caused the bone marrow suppression. A bone marrow biopsy confirmed his suspicion, and he sought care from a highly recommended hematologist at the University Hospitals in Minneapolis. He was admitted to the hospital, placed on the newest, best treatment protocol, and then, with nothing else left to do, he settled in to wait for his bone marrow to recover. Unfortunately, the days stretched into weeks without any change in his blood counts. His mood became darker as his hopes for a quick recovery dimmed. He wanted desperately to be back on the wards, caring for his own patients. Moreover, he had the burden of knowing he had inadvertently poisoned himself.

The nurses on ward 6B said he was both smart and intuitive. But he had become progressively more difficult to please as time went on and he became more frustrated. He would allow anyone attempting to draw his blood only one chance, dismissing them abruptly if they failed. During my time on 6B, Dr. Hanson also dismissed the intern on service, something that had never happened before, apparently clashing with him over issues of care.

I remember walking past his room while on my rounds with other patients. His face was always turned away from the door, his gaze intently fixed on the window by his bed. My own attending physician, Dr. Jones, pulled me aside one morning after rounds. "Have you heard about Dr. Hanson," he asked, "the intern from Mayo?" I nodded my head. "He has requested a transfer to another medicine service, but I'd like to keep him here with me on 6B. Do you think you can handle it?"

My heart jumped. I was the only female physician and intern on the medicine service right now, and I feared this patient might be trouble. As one of only two women in the internal medicine program that year, I was trying to keep a low profile (if that was possible!). Female physicians were still uncommon in the 1970s; my medical school class was considered pioneering because it was 6 percent women. We were excited and eager, but we knew we'd be carefully scrutinized. After graduating from medical school to the grind of residency, we often found ourselves somewhat alone. Sometimes I would hang out at the nurses' station for the feminine companionship, though usually, I was too tired to care. Like all pioneers, we had to earn the right to be there, to take our place as physicians alongside the men, as peers and colleagues.

"Sure I can handle him," I said with confidence I didn't feel. "And I'm good with a needle, too!"

The attending physician looked at me with a slightly puzzled glance. "Can you handle the disease?" he asked firmly. "He has aplastic anemia."

"Certainly I can," I answered promptly, then paused slightly. "I understand Dr. Hanson only gives one chance to draw his blood," I added with a smile.

"Better get it the first time then, Dr. Amatuzio!" Dr. Jones said crisply.

"Right, thank you, I will!" I said as I turned to gather that morning's charts.

"I will inform Dr. Hanson he will remain on my service then," Dr. Jones said as he walked away, "and that *you* will be his intern." I took a deep breath as I watched him go.

After lunch, I sat down at the nurses' station to review my new patient's chart. His reasons for being demanding seemed clear. Blood draws were ordered twice each day, morning and evening, to monitor his blood counts. And a bone marrow biopsy, an uncomfortable procedure, was performed each week to check the results of a promising new but still experimental therapy, anti-lymphocyte globulin, or ALG, a treatment that proved useful for many with aplastic anemia. Dr. Hanson had been in the hospital for two months now, with no indication of bone marrow recovery, an ominous sign. My heart went out to him even before we met. How unfair, I thought, to get so sick at such an important time in life. (Of course, now I realize *every* time in life is important.)

Still, I procrastinated, walking past his half-closed door three or four times that afternoon, waiting until his visitors had gone and until the evening blood draw was due. I recognized several of his guests as physicians; I hoped they had cheered his mood.

When the time came, I pulled my hair back neatly in a ponytail, straightened my shirt and name tag, and filled my white-coat pockets with the necessary needles, syringes, and blood tubes; I wanted to look as professional as possible. Dr. Hanson's room was quiet; it was late afternoon, with the January sky quickly darkening. I knocked softly and walked in and stood there a moment. "Dr. Hanson, my name is Dr. Amatuzio, Janis. I'm your new doc, the intern on red medicine."

He didn't move, or even acknowledge my words, his gaze fixed on the window.

I moved quietly to the foot of his bed and then walked slowly around it to the window side of the room. A small bedside lamp cast a faint glow onto the bed, outlining a handsome face with strong young features and big brown eyes. The sheets were pulled down to just above his waist; I couldn't help notice his still-muscular arms, gaunt chest and abdomen, and smooth, slightly pale skin. He didn't look like most physicians; he was handsome in such a rugged way. But I also noticed the bruises on his hands and arms marking the sites where blood had been drawn. I quickly surveyed his forearms and spotted a vein that I knew I could use. When I glanced back at his face, I realized he was studying me, and I felt my cheeks turn red. He seemed pleased with my sudden discomfort.

"I'm Janis," I said simply.

"I heard you the first time," he replied flatly.

I studied his face for a brief moment, feeling the force of his frustration. "Let's get your blood drawn, and then we can talk. I'm good at this, Dr. Hanson," I offered quietly.

"Sure you are. You've got a chance, one chance," he said as he unfolded his arm.

I took a long look and palpated gently. I took the tourniquet out of my pocket and laid the small blue-topped blood tube on the bed beside him. He turned away, and I quickly inserted a 23-gauge butterfly needle under the skin, immediately hitting the vein. He didn't move a muscle.

"Done," I said quietly, as I released the tourniquet and held a piece of cotton firmly over the puncture site for a few minutes to prevent further bruising.

"Really?" he asked, with a hint of surprise in his voice. "You got it the first time? I didn't feel it!"

"Good," I said, holding up the tube of blood "So you'll keep me till tomorrow?" I added with a half smile.

"That bad, huh?"

"The word is you fired your last G1," I said, using hospital jargon for "intern."

"Sure did. Being here is bad enough without some arrogant jerk that can't even draw blood getting defensive with me!"

"Oh..."

"The last one thought he knew everything," he continued, "and thank God I only had the guy before that for three days before he rotated off service. He didn't know any hematology *or* medicine."

"This has got to be tough for you," I said with a sigh.

"Tougher than you'll ever know."

"I'll run this blood down to the lab and stop back with the results, if you'd like," I offered.

"I'd like that; I'd like it a lot. Thanks."

"See you later, then," I said as I left the room and headed for the hematology lab.

And that was the way we worked it for the rest of the time I was on that rotation. With his consent, and that of the attending physician, Dr. Jones, I personally started drawing all the daily blood tests, and doing it only once each day, late in the afternoon. Then I would report the results to both of them before I went home in the evening. Jeff and I would discuss his progress, the significance of his blood counts, and often the weather, for he was an avid outdoorsman. Over the next weeks and months I learned a lot about him, and I met his wife and young son, as well as many of his friends and other family members.

I RECALL VIVIDLY one snowy Saturday evening in February. I was on call that evening and visiting hours were over. I was feeling good since my resident had given me the following day off. The wards had quieted down, my patients were stable, and I had waited till Jeff's nightly visitors left before I stopped in with the results of his cell counts. Unfortunately, the red and white cell counts still hovered at the low end of the normal range.

"So, I hear you have a day off tomorrow," he said.

I was surprised that he knew. "I do," I said slowly, looking closely at his face. "This is my third day off since I started last May; I'm leaving after rounds in the morning."

He looked down, away from my half smile. "What are you going to do?" he asked quietly, then quickly added, "I hope you don't mind my asking." Jeff knew most of my waking and sleeping hours were spent right there on 6B, and I was acutely aware of his longing to walk out of the hospital healthy and get back to his beloved outdoors.

"Oh, I thought I might go cross-county skiing, maybe down on Pike's Island near Fort Snelling. on the Mississippi. It's supposed to be pretty nice outside tomorrow."

I was sitting on a chair next to his bed; he looked at me and put his hand on mine. What he said next I will never forget.

"Janis, ski for me tomorrow, will you? And come back and..." His eyes welled up with tears, and so did mine.

I held his hand tightly, and his gaze, for a long moment and answered, "Jeff, I'll ski for *you* tomorrow, and I'll come back and tell you about every step of the way." He nodded and we sat there without another word, looking out the window at the snowflakes spinning and dancing outside his hospital room.

While I don't remember much about the other days off that year, I do remember that one, vividly. I left the hospital by 10 A.M. and was down on the island by noon. The sky was a bright winter blue, and several inches of fresh snow blanketed the ground, sparkling and swirling in the sunlight and wind. Pike's Island is part of Fort Snelling State Park, nestled on the banks of the Mississippi River below an old fort dating from the 1800s. The island is connected to the rest of the park by a narrow walkway and wooden bridge. Not many visitors use the park in the winter, just those on cross-country skis.

I tucked my sandwich and water bottle inside my jacket, strapped on my skis, and grabbed my poles. The snow squeaked under the new ski wax, and I pushed hard against my poles, wanting to feel my muscles ache so I could forget about all the sick people and long hours I had faced that year. My mind shifted to the rhythm of the skis and the sound of my breath in the crisp air. Finally I pushed the hospital away for a little while.

When I rounded the southern tip of the island an hour later, I could see ice floes scattered against the riverbanks like a deck of cards casually tossed across a table. I stopped there for a moment to catch my breath, aware of how good it felt to move and how comfortably warm, happy, and carefree I felt. I soaked up the sight of the river and the sound of its current, below the ice. I could almost feel the deep, barely audible rush and push of the water against the frozen banks. The occasional sharp crack and groan of the ice near the open water caught me off guard. The river and the park filled my senses and seemed to vibrate and shimmer with life itself.

I must have stood there longer than I realized, because I felt my skin start to chill in the winter air. Time to start moving again, I thought and stretched myself back into the rhythm of the day, lost in the sunlight that turned snow to diamonds, tracing the tracks of deer and rabbit, feeling the gaze of the trees and birds, skiing for Jeff Hanson and for myself.

Late the next Monday afternoon, with blood counts in hand, I stopped to see the man who had asked me to ski for him. We discussed his care and counts; then he looked at me expectantly, and I began recounting every detail of my afternoon on Pike's Island. He listened intently and then asked about the smell of the air, the types of trees and tracks on the ground, and the clouds in the sky.

"Did you see anyone else?"

"No, not a soul," I answered, "but I didn't feel alone. It was as though I could feel every animal in the forest and could hear the river breathing. It was an amazing day."

He held up his hand and nodded with a faint smile. "So you felt it," he said; "you felt it in your soul." His voice drifted off, and I felt as though part of him left the room. "That was what I felt like last summer in the woods up north, when I was building my cabin. I was up there mostly alone but I wasn't lonely. As the days passed, I felt like I had my hand on the pulse of the earth. And I sensed the rhythm, the rhythm of life; I had the forest and the sunlight by day and the northern lights and stars by night. But there was something else: I felt strong inside and out; I felt whole, and deeply connected to life, to God. It's hard to explain, but once you've been there, you can face anything, 'cause you *know* you're safe, you're fine, you're whole."

The afternoon light began to fade. From the corridor came the sound of aides handing out the dinner trays. I just sat there quietly. What he said felt true to me, and I marveled at his words; I just didn't understand as well and as deeply as he did. All the same, I nodded in silence. The moment was his.

WINTER MELTED INTO SPRING, and Jeff's bone marrow and blood counts improved enough for him to go home to his beloved family and friends. We parted joyfully and with a deep sense of accomplishment; he was delighted with his newfound health, and I was pleased I had lasted as his intern and had become his physician. Most of all, I was privileged to call him my friend.

We lost touch with each other, but several years later I learned that he had died the following summer. I grieved his death and miss him still. More than once I have wordlessly thanked him for his honesty and trust, which made me stronger and wiser. Each time a patient died, I felt somehow diminished. I did not have the perspective to understand that perhaps death is a doorway, a doorway home.

I NOW REALIZE THAT THERE are many, many intangible gifts, both given and received, in the long hours, days, and intimate moments in the making of a physician. Those we care for truly point the way. Therein lies the richness.

WITH ALL MY HEART

D oc, am I going to be okay?" Mr. Nelson whispered hesitantly to me as he watched the overhead monitor in the
cardiac catheterization suite. I was perched on a stool near his
head, sandwiched between the IV poles, resuscitative parapher-
nalia, and the anesthesiologist. The year was 1978. I was in the
final months of my internal medicine internship, rotating on
the cardiology service of the heart hospital. The year had been
intense and dramatic, but nothing in my training had prepared
me for the events of that day.

My patient, Andy Nelson, was a smart, confident, forty-six-
year-old pharmacist who had been admitted for "atypical chest
pain." An extensive work-up had revealed no cause for his
symptoms. Coronary artery angiography, then a relatively new
procedure, was proposed to definitively rule out any undetected

heart disease. After consulting with his wife and family, Mr. Nelson chose to go ahead, but he insisted on being awake to watch the monitor during this exciting, novel procedure. His doctors had confidently agreed. As the intern on the cardiology service, I had gathered the initial history and performed the physical examination. Andy Nelson's care was now in the hands of the cardiologists.

My hand reached out under the sterile sheets to meet his. All eyes were fixed on the overhead screen; Dr. Thomas, the cardiology fellow, had steadily threaded the catheter through the access site on the leg into the femoral artery, then on up into the aorta, and finally to the heart. As he skillfully identified and entered the left coronary artery opening, the carefully injected radio-opaque dye lit up the arterial branches like a beautiful oak tree outlined against a winter sky. No abnormalities there. The technology was stunning, and all of us, including my patient, were awestruck by the glimpse of the perfection of the design.

The dimly lit room was filled with the buzz of state-of-the-art electronic devices, and conversation was hushed. The catheter was slowly advanced into the ostium, or opening, of the right coronary artery as we all watched breathlessly. Suddenly an abnormal blush appeared near the catheter tip as it advanced into the right coronary artery. I remember thinking, "What is that?"

My confusion quickly transformed into concern. Disbelief was palpable as the cardiology resident repeated the dye injection. The abnormal blush was unmistakable. "Call the attending — call Sweeney! I want him in here STAT!!" ordered Dr.

Thomas. Dr. Sweeney was the attending staff cardiologist, a competent, well-known, and liked physician.

I could feel Mr. Nelson's palms start to sweat.

"We have extravasated dye, extravascular dye!" shouted Dr. Orland, the third-year resident on the heart service.

"What are his pressure and pulse?" Dr. Thomas requested.

"Pressure steady, pulse regular but rate is increased to 90 to 95 beats per minute," replied the anesthesiologist, Dr. Stone.

"I think the vessel is torn — we have a perforation!" Dr. Orland exclaimed.

Just then Dr. Sweeney strode into the suite, hastily donning a gown and gloves while the angiography nursing staff secured the ties at his waist. I remember my patient's grip tightening on my hand.

"What have we got?" he asked sternly.

"A tear in the right main, at the ostium. It looks like a laceration," Dr. Thomas replied. "I had just advanced the catheter into the base of the right coronary artery and infused a few cc's of dye to be sure I was in the right place, and, well — you can see the blush of dye on the monitor…" His voice trailed off. Catheters in those days were less flexible than those in use now; unfortunately, the catheter tip had torn a hole in the coronary artery, causing blood to spill out into the space around the heart, the pericardial sac.

Dr. Sweeney studied the monitor for a moment and then briskly took charge. "Call the heart-lung bypass team — I want them down here STAT. I want this patient put on bypass immediately. Call the OR — tell them we have a right coronary artery ostium perforation that will need intraoperative

repair, and to clear an operating room for us. Call Dr. Berg —
I need to speak to the cardiovascular staff surgeon on the
phone *now!*"

The room became a blur of frantic activity. The angiography suite was in the heart hospital, adjacent to the main hospital where the operating rooms were located. Mr. Nelson's life would depend on a successful repair of the torn vessel, but it also meant he had to be moved from the angiography suite in the heart hospital to the OR in the adjoining main hospital while on the bypass pump.

I felt lost and a little helpless at that moment, but I was anchored to the spot by Mr. Nelson's hand, which was locked firmly on mine. "Will I be okay?" he asked, looking up at me.

"What?" Even with his hand in mine, I had almost forgotten my patient in the rush and drama in the room.

"Will I be okay?"

"Oh dear," I thought, "What do I say?" — wishing I had more experience, more words, more wisdom...

I looked into his eyes and mustered up my courage. "It can be fixed, Mr. Nelson, but it is serious. Your blood vessel, the right coronary artery, is torn, and you will need immediate surgery." I could see the fear in his eyes. I stumbled and said the only thing I could think of, "I can't tell you for sure how this will come out, but I won't leave your side."

"Thank you, Doctor; that means a lot to me." He paused and with a slightly different look in his eyes, one that hadn't been there moments before, squeezed my hand and said, "I'm scared, but I'm going to get through this." I didn't realize then the degree of courage it took for Andy Nelson to face that situation the way he did. He reminded me of Churchill's description of courage as "grace under pressure."

"Yes, we are going to get through this," I said.

"One more thing, Doc. Do me a favor?"

"Sure, Mr. Nelson, anything," I responded, my face close to his as I knelt down.

"Tell my wife that I love her," he whispered, "with all my heart."

"I will, I promise." I felt the words catch in my throat.

His grip slowly loosened on mine as the anesthesiologist administered medications to relax and anesthetize him. He looked calmer now, though I wasn't sure if it was the medications or his resolve. The pump team arrived and began to work furiously to insert the bypass lines that would allow the blood to bypass the heart and lungs, allowing precious moments for the surgeon to repair the damage. The concern and intense focus of the medical personnel were palpable.

Minutes passed quickly, then suddenly the cardiac monitor began beeping loudly. The heart beat had abruptly gone from its regular rhythm, or normal sinus in medical terminology, into a life-threatening ventricular fibrillation. "V-fib arrest!" shouted Dr. Thomas. "Give me the paddles. Prepare to shock." The nurse pulled down the sheet, exposing Mr. Nelson's bare, pallid chest. Gel was quickly applied, and Dr. Thomas yelled, "Stand back!" as everyone moved away from the cart. Mr. Nelson's chest jumped as the charge was delivered, and all eyes returned to the monitor.

The fibrillation still persisted. "Shocking again!" said Dr. Thomas. "Table clear," responded the staff nurse. Mr. Nelson's chest jumped, and all eyes again returned to the monitor. "Normal sinus rhythm, and we have a blood pressure!" exclaimed Dr. Thomas with relief. Everyone in the room went back to their tasks with renewed intensity and frantically focused activity. I watched the preparations alertly.

"Preparing to transfer to bypass pump," shouted one of the technicians.

The staff crowded around Mr. Nelson's now-still body, filled with tubes and monitors, and I found myself pushed back to the room's edge. "Andy, I'm right here. I'm not leaving," I said silently to my patient as I let go of his hand completely.

All of a sudden, something happened that I still cannot explain. I saw, or more accurately felt, a shimmer of light in the corner of the room above the foot of the angiography table. I quickly looked to see if the pump team was using a lighting device that perhaps reflected off the wall, but they were not. I looked again, somewhat puzzled, and suddenly had the profound sense of a deep, overwhelming, calm presence, in stark contrast to the frantic activity in the room. It was unmistakable! I was amazed. "What is going on?" I thought as I looked again, peering intensely at the ceiling. "Can't anyone else see that? Am I losing my mind?"

As I stared at the glimmer in the corner of the room, an odd thought formed in my mind, and I clearly heard these words, "He's watching...and he's fine!" I didn't know where they came from and didn't fully understand their significance, but they were manifestly clear.

Just then the anesthesiologist shouted, "We've lost him — no pulse, no pressure."

"Start CPR!" ordered Dr. Sweeney. "We're almost on the pump — hold on to him. I'm not going to lose him, not on my watch!"

"Okay! On bypass," the technician shouted as the large machine laced with pumps and vacuum hoses began to hum. I watched as the blood began to fill the chambers rapidly. "Bypass is working," said the cardiac technician. All stood back for a moment as the whir of the machine filled the air, and the tubes and hoses filled with my patient's blood. "What's the blood oxygen saturation?" Dr. Sweeney demanded.

"At 89 percent and climbing... 92 percent, now 95 percent," the technician called out.

"Let's take him to the OR," Dr. Stone ordered. "I need the smallest person here to ride on the cart, to compress his chest once every two minutes." His eyes rapidly scanned the room. "You!" he said pointing at me. I made my way forward and was literally catapulted onto the cart by many hands. I perched on my knees next to Mr. Nelson's torso, my hands clasped one over the other on his mid-sternum. "Compress when I tell you," said the anesthesiologist.

"Okay," I nodded, wide-eyed.

I remember the speed with which we were transported down the hallways. This was before the days of battery packs, and the bypass machine required electrical power. Heavy-duty thick black cords were run down hallways, rapidly plugged and unplugged as we passed by. When we came to the elevator (the OR was up three floors), an extremely muscular man took over, manually operating the bypass pump by turning a crank lever. I watched his extraordinary effort and resolve, and the beads of sweat that formed on his head, neck, and arms as the elevator took what seemed forever to climb three floors. The doors opened, and electricity was quickly restored to the pump.

We were whisked into the OR, and I climbed off the cart. Mr. Nelson's body seemed still and distant. Dr. Berg asked me to scrub in to assist in the surgery, an unusual privilege for an internal medicine intern. He placed my gloved hands on the edge of the draped surgical field as he opened Mr. Nelson's chest. "Don't move unless I tell you," he sternly ordered.

"No, sir, I won't," I responded.

As the minutes turned into hours I felt my feet and lower back began to ache. Dr. Sweeney and the cardiology senior fellow, Dr. Thomas, peeked in frequently to check on our status. The surgery progressed, and the facts began to unfold. The right coronary artery had indeed been torn by the catheter tip used for injecting dye into the artery. This unfortunate medical mistake had caused the sac around the heart to fill with blood, and the heart muscle, deprived of oxygen for too long, had been irreversibly damaged. Despite all extraordinary efforts, Mr. Nelson was pronounced dead on the table, in the OR, three and a half hard hours later.

I COULD FEEL THE FATIGUE and disappointment set in as we ungloved and ungowned. I felt defeated and somehow reluctant to leave Mr. Nelson's lifeless body there in the OR, covered respectfully with a sheet. The room felt empty to me. I felt nothing except my own dismay and numbness at the day's events. However, the hardest task still remained, speaking with Mrs. Nelson, my patient's wife. Dr. Berg and I walked down the hall together; Dr. Thomas had already spoken to her, telling her that he had inadvertently torn the artery. Her anger, grief, and dismay were understandable. Dr. Thomas, too, was devastated and had gone home, too distressed to stay at work.

Other staff members had kept Mrs. Nelson informed during the dramatic rush to the OR and the surgery. She was sitting in a small private surgical waiting room, looking both hopeful and dazed. Her eyes searched ours as we entered the room. "I am so sorry, Mrs. Nelson," Dr. Berg began. "We were unable to save him." I saw the hope leave her eyes as the devastating but not unexpected news finally sank in. Her hands came up to her mouth and then covered her eyes. "We tried everything we knew, but the heart muscle was too badly damaged after the artery was torn. I suspected as much might have happened. The staff here did everything they could," Dr. Berg offered. She nodded and began to weep, big hard sobs. I sat down beside her and put my hand gently on her back. "Do you have any questions about what happened?" he asked.

"No, I can't think of anything else right now," she answered numbly.

"I expect some will come up, given the nature of what happened. You can call me. I'll be here," he said as he got up to go, looking at me.

"I'll stay with her awhile," I said. Dr. Berg nodded and left the room, closing the door behind him.

"Do you have anyone to be with you?" I asked.

"My sister is on her way; she is flying in. I expect her here any moment," she replied. She openly wept as the next few moments passed. My heart ached as I sat there quietly; I struggled hard to keep back my own tears.

"I do have a question," she said hesitantly. "Were you there with him?"

"Yes," I replied, "I never left his side, literally." Then I proceeded to tell her of the day's events, as much for me as for her, I suspect. I told her how I held his hand in the cath lab when we both saw the extravasated dye, how I rode on the cart kneeling next to him and pumped his chest on the trip to the OR. I told her about the muscular man who pumped the heart-lung machine by hand when we were on the elevator for what seemed an eternity. I told her how I stood next to the surgeon for hours as he valiantly attempted the vascular repair.

She clung to my every word. When I finished, she said, "Oh, thank you for that, thank you so much."

"And there is something else. He asked me to tell you something," I said, suddenly remembering. She looked up at me, her eyes now focused intently on mine. "When we were in the cath lab and realized that something had gone wrong, he asked me to tell you something."

"Yes?" she said expectantly.

I took a deep breath, "Your husband said he was determined to get through this and then asked me to tell you specifically that he loves you . . . with all his heart." I barely choked the words out; the emotion of the day overwhelmed me. Then we both sat there, awash in tears.

She looked up. "When did he say that?"

"Just before they put him out; before hooking him up to the bypass machine," I replied. We were silent for a moment.

"I am still so stunned," she said at last. "I can hardly believe this has happened. He was so smart and so sure this would go well. He told me not to worry. He said he would be watching . . . and he would be fine."

With those words, two things happened simultaneously: I felt a shiver go down my back as I remembered my experience of the shimmering light at the end of the cart, the peaceful presence in the cath lab, and the words that had formed in my mind.

The door to the waiting room suddenly burst open as her sister and family arrived. I quietly excused myself as they embraced and wept, and I walked down the hall to the empty women's locker room. "Maybe he really *was* watching . . ." I thought.

I never spoke to Mrs. Nelson again, and I didn't think much about that unusual happening until years later. It has only been with time and experience that I have begun trusting myself to make meaning out of these unexplainable happenings. Back then I was working too hard to dwell on much of anything.

DAUNTING DECISIONS

Shortly after Mr. Nelson died, I received a notice that my next two-month clinical rotation was scheduled in the emergency department and would be split between two places: two weeks at the University Hospitals ER followed by six weeks at a busy trauma center, the Hennepin County Medical Center ER. I was delighted, even though I had hoped to spend all eight weeks at Hennepin County. The fast pace of that ER would be very different from the University Hospitals ER, and a welcome change, I thought, from the many chronically ill and diagnostically difficult patients I had been treating.

By now it was early spring and I was nearing the end of my internship. Soon I would have to decide whether to continue my residency training in internal medicine or pursue pathology. Although my thoughts occasionally returned to Dr. Osterberg and forensic pathology, I was happy with my current choice, keenly focused both on my internal medicine training and on mastering disease. But the next two weeks would change my life completely.

Those first days in the emergency room at the "U," I quickly learned my main role: stabilize and triage. In fact, our ER felt more like an after-hours admissions clinic since the true emergencies bypassed us for the major trauma centers. The acutely and chronically ill patients who rolled through our doors were usually not "true emergencies" and were quickly admitted to the hospital proper by their attending staff physicians, who jealously guarded their referrals. In the first week I learned more about politics than medicine. Then everything changed.

On Saturday afternoon as I returned from lunch, the head nurse notified me that an oncology patient who had been discharged from University Hospitals that same day had suffered an apparent cardiac arrest in the ambulance while being transported home. The ambulance crew had radioed in that they had turned around and were speeding back. They were now ten minutes out and racing for our door.

"An oncology patient," I said. "Do you know any other details?"

The nurse shook her head. "No."

The senior resident was manning the phone line with the ambulance crew, calling out orders for IV medications, including epinephrine, bicarbonate, and lidocaine, medications used to start and stabilize the heart. He was attempting to interpret the cardiac rhythms reported by the ambulance crew. (This was before the days of more sophisticated telemetry and monitoring techniques.) I quickly worked with the staff to prepare the "stab room," or stabilization room — and then we waited anxiously. The minutes seemed like hours, and our own hearts were racing.

When the ambulance arrived, everyone sprang into action. The back doors of the ambulance flew open, and we pulled our unconscious patient, a slender, frail-looking middle-aged woman, onto the cart. The paramedics continued CPR as we ran, pushing the cart into the stab room. I pushed out of my mind the thought that this patient looked vaguely familiar.

The senior resident shouted orders in rapid-fire succession. "CVP line, blood pressure, EKG, Ringers Lactate wide open, blood gases, electrolytes, STAT!" We all jumped to comply, working furiously.

"We've got V-fib!" he shouted suddenly. "Paddles! *Clear!* Shocking now!" Everyone leaped back from the table. The woman's chest jumped as the electrical current flowed through her, and all eyes fixed on the cardiac monitor. The restored rhythm slowed, then returned to the deadly fibrillation. "Bicarb, epi, STAT. *Clear!* Shocking *now!*" The wild fluttering on the cardiac monitor paused, then seemed to shudder as it reorganized itself into a slow but normal sinus rhythm.

"Is she perfusing? Do you feel a pulse?" the senior resident shouted as he peered intently at the paramedic.

The paramedic slowly shook his head "No, no palpable pulse."

We all continued to work furiously, racing against time and luck. In all the frenzied activity, I hadn't really looked at her face, hadn't let that glimmer of recognition back into my mind. And then, I don't quite know how it happened, but I did see her face, and my gut literally lurched. I suddenly realized this was Lilly Hancock, *my* patient from 5 West! I had rotated off the oncology service only a week ago. I felt all upside-down and sick to my stomach.

"Rhythm?" the senior resident demanded.

"Normal sinus with two short runs of V-tach, still nonperfusing," the nurse anesthetist said, referring to the irregularity.

"*Damn it!*" came the hissed response.

Just at that moment, the head nurse pulled back the thin curtain to the room, her voice loud and stern. "Doctor! I just spoke to the patient's husband. She has metastatic lung cancer, and she is a *no code*. I repeat, *no code!*"

A moment of disbelief clouded the room. "What?" yelled the senior resident.

"She is DNR," said the nurse firmly, referring to the patient's "do not resuscitate" wishes.

"Are you *sure?*" asked one of the paramedics.

"I just spoke to her husband, the legal next of kin," the nurse repeated. "Mr. Hancock wanted us to know her wishes."

Unknown to me, Lilly and her husband had decided against any heroics; they had signed the "do not resuscitate" directive the day before she left the hospital.

LILLY HANCOCK *DID* HAVE LUNG CANCER, a type known as small-cell carcinoma of the lung. This diagnosis surprised me because I knew she had never smoked a cigarette in her life. She had been followed for years at University Hospitals for a rare benign blood disorder, but her cancer was not diagnosed until she began to lose weight, almost twenty pounds, without trying. By then, unfortunately, it had already spread to her bones.

She was admitted to 5 West, where she became my patient. A chest X-ray, lung biopsy, bone scan, and bone biopsy told the rest of the story. The tumor had started in her left lung and spread to her bone marrow. She was courageous when I told her the diagnosis and decided to pursue chemotherapy, the only real option left to her.

She had developed pneumonia while she was hospitalized, and I had treated her vigorously with antibiotics. I remember her as a kind, loving mother and wife, and she wanted everything done so she could return home soon, to be with her family for whatever time she had left. She had come so close to getting her wish.

IN THE ER THE SENIOR RESIDENT acknowledged the nurse's announcement. "Okay, folks! That's it, then. Stop the resuscitation immediately." We all backed away from the table slightly. He looked at the clock on the wall. "Time of death, 13:20 hours..." He looked at us and said, "Thanks for your help." The staff took a collective sigh and, one by one, turned away.

But I stayed in the room, stunned and dismayed. I didn't want to leave Lilly's side and wouldn't let the nurse pull the sheet over her face. "Not yet," I said. "Not yet!" as I folded it at her neck. "Her husband is coming, isn't he?" I asked.

"Yes, he is on his way."

"Well, he won't want to look at her with a sheet over her

head," I said with a sense of dismay in my voice. The nurse quietly left the room.

Moments later my senior resident walked back in and looked at the scene. I was still standing there. "What's wrong, Janis?"

I struggled for a moment and then blurted out, "She might have had cancer, but she was doing fine. I know, because she was my patient!" Tears began to roll down my face. "And she just wanted to go home! We shouldn't have stopped the resuscitation!"

Many things could have happened at that moment, but I am so grateful for what actually did happen. He stepped over to me, gently placed his hand on my shoulder, and guided me down the hall to the residents' room. We closed the door, and he sat there and compassionately waited, letting me cry.

"Your first week in the ER, your first ER code, and it's *your* patient. I am so sorry, Janis. I am so sorry." I remember studying the floor, searching for words that just didn't come. "We did the right thing, Janis, letting her go...and respecting her husband's wishes. She had terminal cancer."

"I know," I acknowledged. But I felt such a deep sadness inside; it just didn't seem right.

"Why don't you take the rest of the day off, go home, and get some rest," he offered.

"Thank you. I think I will," I said wearily.

I DIDN'T REALIZE IT AT THAT MOMENT, but Lilly Hancock's death was a turning point for me. It may have been the timing or my fatigue, or something else. But after that, I seriously turned my attention to pathology and to forensic pathology in particular.

I had a long talk with my father about my feelings, the events of that day, and my patient, Lilly Hancock. He listened carefully and thoughtfully and then encouraged my interest in pathology.

"Take a break from internal medicine and give it a try," he said. "Now is the time to find out, and besides, some of the best doctors I know were trained in pathology as well." He also suggested I speak with Dr. Richard Ebert, the director of my internal medicine department at the University Hospitals. Dr. Ebert and my father were longtime friends and associates. When I called the next week to make an appointment, Dr. Ebert received me warmly. As I explained my interest in pathology as well as what happened with Lilly Hancock, he listened intently.

"I know Don Amatuzio quite well, and I know he always loved pathology. He was quite good at it," he said. "I even expect he encouraged you to take that pathology rotation at Hennepin County Hospital during medical school."

I glanced down with a smile. "No, Dr. Ebert, he didn't 'encourage' me. He *told* me I would take it."

"Well, your father always did have a way with words, as well as a desire to learn. What an incredible lifelong student he has been! And unfortunately we often lose our best doctors to pathology," he said with a smile.

"I studied with Dr. Robert Anderson, Dr. Cal Bandt, Dr. Kenny Osterberg, and Dr. John Coe during my pathology rotation," I noted. Dr. Coe was the highly respected and nationally known director of the department of pathology at the Hennepin

County Medical Center in Minneapolis, as well as the Hennepin County medical examiner. Dr. Bandt was one of his first pathology residents and also studied forensic medicine under Dr. Coe. Later Dr. Bandt went on to direct the hospital laboratory, establish the forensic toxicology laboratory, and do pioneering research in postmortem chemistry, the study of changes in the blood and body fluids to reveal the cause and time of death.

"Sounds like you met some of the brightest physicians in pathology. However, I have to warn you, three of them are forensic pathologists!"

"I know they are but..." I said quickly, "it was just so interesting."

He nodded and leaned forward, "I'll give you a year to decide, a year's leave of absence from the program, Janis. But one thing — let me know your decision by next spring. And greet your father for me."

"I will," I said with a smile. "I will!"

"I suspect you two are a lot alike!" he answered. "Maybe more than you know." But he offered no explanation of this puzzling comment, just stood up and walked me to the office door.

Days later, I sat in Dr. Coe's office at the Hennepin County Medical Center, which was located in the medical examiner's office even though he still practiced surgical pathology and took calls from the clinical laboratory. I remember sitting on the big black couch across from his desk. My eyes seemed to barely reach over the desktop, so I sat up as tall as I could.

"Certainly you can do forensic pathology, Janis. But you will have to do four years of anatomic and clinical pathology as well. The forensic fellowship is an additional year of study after that." He must have seen my disappointment because he added, "But we might be able to give you some exposure to forensics as we go along."

"That would be just fine with me, Dr. Coe. I really feel this is the field I'm going to pursue."

"Good, then. Fill out the paperwork, and I'll speak to the others in the department."

As it turned out, Dr. Coe was as good as his word, and I didn't have to wait four years to begin my forensic studies. Although I started my pathology training in the summer of 1978, a position in the fellowship program opened up for the 1979–80 year, just one year later. I was the first woman ever to be accepted into the fellowship program. But that was still in the future.

Several weeks later I received my acceptance letter from the Hennepin County Department of Pathology. I proudly started my pathology residency that July. I was delighted with my decision and the studies. Some months later, I visited Dr. Ebert to tell him I would be staying in pathology. He smiled and nodded his head with understanding. "I am not surprised, Janis! I know you'll do well. Tell your father I understand."

I looked at him for a moment, then said simply, "I will." And quickly forgot all about it. It wasn't until almost thirty years later that I learned from my mother the surprising meaning behind his cryptic words.

After rereading yet another draft of this book, my dear mother happened to comment on the parallels between my decision and Dad's. "You know," she said in a phone conversation one evening, "almost the same thing happened to your father when he was in residency."

"Really?" I asked.

"Yes," she answered, "it was after World War II. He was at the Veterans Hospital in Minneapolis in his residency. It was before you were born."

"What happened?"

"One of his patients died after he performed a procedure. Your father was devastated and almost quit medicine! But I think you should talk to him about it."

Later one afternoon while I was visiting my parents, I asked my father about that event. His reply astonished me in many ways, but most of all, it comforted me to know that I wasn't alone in my anguish or my choices.

He told me that after returning home from Japan, he began a subspecialty training in chest and heart disease at the VA Hospital under Dr. Bill Tucker and Dr. Abe Falk. Richard Ebert and my father were in the same residency class, and they became good friends. My father recalled that a handsome young man was admitted to Ward 62 for treatment of tuberculosis, which he had contracted while stationed in Guam during the war. A chest X-ray revealed an abscess in the right lung. My father consulted with the staff physician, and they decided to drain the pus from the young veteran's chest. After my father placed the needle in the abscess, the purulent material began draining through the chest wall.

Then, unfortunately, the man began to cough violently. The needle dislodged from the abscess, which caused air and pus to enter the bloodstream. The patient became unconscious and had a seizure. Despite all of my father's efforts, his patient died.

Quietly, and with remorse still in his voice, my now eighty-eight-year-old father told me he had been completely devastated. He talked to the young man's family, then went immediately up to see the program chair, Dr. C. J. Watson, and abruptly resigned from medicine.

"Your father stayed home for three days," my mother said from the doorway of my father's library. "I remember it well." She turned to look directly at her husband. "You just sat there at home, so down and depressed, doing nothing but blaming yourself for that young man's death . . . until Dr. Watson called that next evening."

"Yes, I remember that call like it was yesterday," my father said. "Dr. Watson was so kind, and he asked me to come back to medicine. He said the young man's death was not my fault, that these accidents happen despite all the best efforts of the people involved, but it took me a long time to get over it! He asked me to take some time off from the medicine service and work in the pathology research laboratory, in the biochemistry section with Dr. Wally Armstrong, the chair of that department."

"What did you do?" I asked.

"I did just what he told me to!" my father answered with a smile. "I went back to work with Dr. Armstrong in the laboratory. He was such a kind man, a big Texan with a wonderful Texas drawl. Dr. Watson must have talked to him, because the first day I started, he sat me down and made me relax. Told me about the patients he'd treated over the years, how some of the same things had happened to him. When he got done talking,

I remember, he took a big Bowie knife out of his pocket. He reached over, plucked a long hair off my arm, and split it in two! Then he leaned over to me, paused, and said that practicing medicine could be compared to splitting a hair. Both are very difficult to do and take practice, precision, and some risk. There were always two ways to look at every experience; the choice was mine. He told me to remember it takes great courage and risk to accomplish great things, and to remember my intention had never been to harm that young man.

"We did good work over the next few years. Some of the methods we researched are still used in the clinical laboratory today. I felt reassured and eventually regained my confidence. And my good friend Richard Ebert always encouraged me, just like he encouraged you, Janis. And after a year or two, I eventually went back to my first love, internal medicine. And you, Janis, went on to yours, forensic pathology."

Now I really saw the truth of the matter. While writing this book, I realized profoundly how my father's path and mine had mirrored each other. Our feelings and choices were too similar for me to think they were just coincidence, even though the events themselves were separated by over thirty years.

Perhaps unconsciously, I took my dad's concerns and mine about the death of our patients to another level. Almost by accident, it seemed, I discovered forensic pathology, the field that allowed me to find answers and peace amid the sadness and despair that haunted me over my patients' deaths during my training in medicine. My father had inadvertently guided me back to my own truth and to his when he insisted I study pathology, *the basis of medicine.*

PART II

THE FIRST SECRET
TRUST YOURSELF

Trust yourself; you'll know.

— CAL BANDT, MD

TRUST YOURSELF

I started my pathology residency at Hennepin County Hospital on a hot summer day, July 1, 1978. The cool basement pathology office seemed both welcome and familiar. I felt relieved, thinking it would be easier to practice forensic pathology than internal medicine, thinking that at least my patients were not dying in my care. I even imagined I would have less responsibility. I had much to learn.

I had many superb teachers in forensic medicine; one in particular stands out in my mind: Dr. Calvin Bandt, who served as assistant chief medical examiner as well as the chief of the hospital clinical laboratory. He taught not only medicine but quite a lot about life and living. There was a steady quality about him, and he always seemed to be there whenever I encountered a difficult diagnostic situation in the morgue or in the lab.

At the outset, I mentally prepared myself to study general pathology, expecting that I would not be able to get into forensics for several years. In addition to Dr. Bandt, Dr. Kenny Osterberg also served as an assistant medical examiner, and both of them took weekend and weeknight calls. Part of their duties included accompanying the death investigators to the scenes of suspicious deaths, those thought to be possible homicides.

Ordinarily I would not have been allowed to go along on such calls, but late in the fall of 1978, Dr. Osterberg suffered a major stroke. Unfortunately, he had had untreated hypertension, which caused the rupture of a blood vessel and resulted in extensive brain damage. I remember that Dr. Coe called me into his office shortly thereafter. Dr. Bandt was there, too, listening as Dr. Coe offered me Dr. Osterberg's on-call position as a deputy medical examiner. I eagerly and immediately accepted and was thrilled beyond words. Little did I know what I was getting myself into...

My very first call as a deputy medical examiner was to a suspicious-death scene in January 1979. As I raced to the medical examiner's office to ride out in the rig with the ME crew that night, my excitement began to fade and be replaced by quivers of apprehension as I quickly realized I knew nothing at all about death scene investigation. The case was reported as an apparent homicide of a taxicab driver in the "projects," a crime-ridden neighborhood in north Minneapolis. Wet, heavy snow was falling rapidly, and the law enforcement officers at the scene were encouraging us to hurry because evidence, including the footprints of the prime suspect, was rapidly being covered.

When we pulled up at the scene, the investigator, Keith, and his assistant grabbed their gear and cameras and trudged up the sidewalk in the rapidly falling snow to meet with the officer in charge. I followed closely behind, mindful of evidence and careful to step only where they did.

The taxi was stopped on the side of the street, with both the driver's and the passenger's doors open. The driver was slumped to his left side with his head down, his body partially resting on the door frame. Blood from an apparent gunshot wound to the back of the head covered his face and chest. Keith started to take photographs, and when he finished, he conferred with the crime lab technicians and together they searched for a driver's license or other form of identification. After they finished and all the photographic documentation was done, Keith nodded at me to approach the body to examine it for rigor and livor, the postmortem changes that aid in determination of time of death. I had been standing quietly on the sidewalk, out of the way. I will never forget what happened next.

A big burly officer with sergeant's stripes on his sleeve stepped in front of me, blocking my path. "You!" he said with authority in his voice.

I looked up, startled. "Yes?"

"Get out of here, Toots! Now!"

"But I'm the deputy medical examiner, and I have to examine this body," I said with disbelief in my voice.

"You're the deputy medical examiner?!" he said with even greater disbelief. At that point Keith stepped up and confirmed my identity. "Sergeant, this is Dr. Amatuzio, our new deputy

ME; she took Dr. Osterberg's place." The sergeant gingerly extended his hand to me, and I shook it cautiously. The other officers were all staring at us, and I felt acutely uncomfortable. The sergeant then stepped aside, grumbling under his breath and shaking his head. "What's this world coming to!" is all I overheard.

I felt shaken up by the incident; it hadn't hit me until then that I was the first female deputy ME at the office — actually the first female deputy ever!

I proceeded to examine the body, in spite of the comment, the rapidly falling snow, and the fact that all eyes were now on me. I knelt down and could see what appeared to be an entrance gunshot wound on the back of the right side of the head. It was caked in blood and partially covered with snow.

"So what caliber gun was used, Doc?" another officer asked.

"What caliber gun?" I repeated.

"Can't you tell from the wound, Doc?"

I paused and felt the blood rush to my face and embarrassment fill my heart. Fortunately, Keith jumped into the conversation. "Oh, the Doc thinks we'd better make that determination back at the morgue, where we can take a better look." I looked up at him gratefully. "Let's get his hands bagged and get transport rolling," he said without pausing. I stepped back and watched the others work.

The ride back to the morgue in the rig was quiet. I thanked Keith for helping me out of that situation. "They do that to all the new guys, Doc. Don't take it personally."

Later the following day, I told Dr. Bandt what had happened at the scene and asked how to tell the caliber of the bullet from the appearance of the wound. "Oh, so they pulled that old trick on you," he said. "Tell them that nobody makes that determination at the scene. The only thing you can say is whether it is large caliber or small." But when I came to the part about "Toots," he almost started to laugh — and I almost started to cry. When he realized I was upset, he put his hand on my shoulder. "Janis, those guys have just never seen a woman at the scene before — I bet none of them have ever seen a woman physician before, except on TV. You just surprised the heck out of them."

"Well, they surprised the heck out of me!" I said.

"Janis, just do your job the best you can out there and here in the office. Be professional, be smart, and be kind. They may not like the fact that you are a girl, but they'll respect the work you do, and that means they'll respect you, too. Have patience, Janis. You'll do just fine."

Dr. Bandt's calm manner and reassuring words made a difference to me. I felt better and regained a small measure of confidence and composure. It wasn't the last time something like that happened to me, but it got easier and sometimes even humorous as time passed.

MUCH AS WITH MY INTERNSHIP, a cancellation in the forensic fellowship program allowed me a head start on my twelve-month forensic fellowship the following year, and also as with my internship, the pace, intensity, and hours were grueling. But the chance to solve the mystery, to uncover the secrets, to speak for the dead fascinated me. I believe that is the reason forensic pathology fascinates so many.

I remember puzzling over the cause of death of a seventy-two-year-old man who had been admitted to a local hospital. The day before, while driving to visit his wife in the hospital, he had collided with a parked car at slow speed. He was evaluated at a local ER and sent home. His daughter found him the next morning, disoriented and confused. Head injuries were suspected, and he was admitted to the hospital. Despite negative X-rays and scans, his condition rapidly worsened, and he died several hours later. Because of the possibility of injury, his death was referred to the medical examiner.

I performed the autopsy the following day, discovering no head injuries, only slight edema (fluid) in the lungs, and mild heart disease. Routine toxicology and a blood alcohol were negative; I was at a loss.

Dr. Bandt was walking past my office where I was intently studying the glass tissue slides from the autopsy under the microscope.

"Dr. Bandt?" I said cautiously. "Would you have a moment to look at this case with me?"

"I'd be happy to!" he said as he strode into my office and sat down at the double-headed teaching microscope. Dr. Bandt was simply brilliant, and he loved forensic pathology and toxicology. He was one of my best teachers, and he especially enjoyed a challenging case. "What have you got here?" he asked. I relayed the history and autopsy findings, negative toxicology, and my growing concern over not discovering a diagnosis.

He listened carefully as his practiced eye scanned the glass microscope slide prepared from tissue samples taken at the autopsy. He smoothly slipped them onto the stage of the scope.

"What do you know about this guy?" he asked. "And why was his wife in the hospital?"

"Retired, living with his daughter since his wife was diagnosed with cancer," I replied.

"So that's what he was depressed about," he said as he reached for the polarizing lenses on my desk — lenses used to aid in looking for foreign substances or abnormal proteins in a tissue sample.

"I didn't get any history that he was depressed," I replied, mystified. I peered again into the microscope. Dr. Bandt was studying a section of kidney. When he placed the polarizing lenses on the stage, the tissue lit up with the reflection of thousands of little crystals, each shaped like a sheaf of wheat. "Calcium oxalate crystals," I said slowly, "the metabolite of ethylene glycol! He must have drunk antifreeze!"

And so the story began to unfold. My patient, distressed over his wife's illness and rattled by the collision, had poisoned himself in a moment of despair. "How did you know that?" I asked.

Dr. Bandt paused. "Well, Janis, study and experience."

It seemed like a long time passed, with Dr. Bandt quietly lost in thought. I even wondered if he had forgotten me sitting there. Several minutes passed as I busied myself by looking at the kidney tissue under the scope.

"When you do this long enough, you'll start to see the patterns, too," he finally said and got up and walked to the door.

"I hope so," I said glumly and mostly to myself.

He stopped in the doorway, and his eyes softened slightly. "Here's one of the secrets to practicing forensic medicine: it's about 50 percent what you know and 50 percent what you feel. That's why you have to keep an open mind — that's when you notice that gut feeling. Study hard and learn everything you can, and then listen to your feelings." I think I took a deep breath at that moment. "Trust yourself, Janis; you'll know." Then he was gone out the door.

Those were probably the most important words of advice Dr. Bandt ever gave me.

THE PRISM

There have been times when I worried whether or not I *could* figure out what "really happened." Then I began to realize that I not only had to trust myself, but also had to trust the process and have the confidence to know that I *would* figure it out. Investigations have taught me the value of making observations, not judgments. There's a difference. The first allows for infinite possibilities; the latter closes the door to all but a handful of conclusions. Additionally, each investigation is as unique as the life of the person who has died; perhaps that is what makes it so interesting. It is also what can make it so difficult.

Making astute observations is like being handed a few small pieces of a puzzle. Then, the observer, with skill and sometimes with an intuitive leap, sees patterns of injury, habits, or symptoms of a disease become clearer, and the whole picture emerges. The observer, the investigator, becomes like a lens in a beam of light, allowing the patterns to converge to a diagnosis, a point of truth or clarity, which is a very important fact when one is investigating life.

IT WAS A COOL, WINDY SUNDAY AFTERNOON. I had just arrived home from the hospital and stepped inside the house when my pager went off — again. A familiar phone number belonging to one of my death investigators came up on the lime green screen, followed by an ominous 911.

"Oh, dear!" I thought as I dialed the number.

After just one ring, the voice of my investigator, Roger Foss, came on the line. "Sorry to bother you, Doc, but I'm at a scene that worries me. I think you better come."

"What do you have, Roger?"

"A call came in to dispatch reporting a man injured in a barn. The first officer on the scene canceled the ambulance and called for backup. The fellow was dead, collapsed in the machine shed. There's blood everywhere, Doc; it really looks suspicious. Crime lab is on the way."

"Okay, I'll be right out. Where are you located?"

"Out County Road 24, two miles past the old creamery on the left. It's a place called Rainbow Farms. You'll see the sign out front. An older man named Harold Olson runs the place — he used to sell vegetables 'til his wife died several years back."

"I should be there in a half hour or so. See you then," I responded as I hung up the phone.

I quickly changed my clothes and grabbed my investigator

bag. "Better take my boots, too," I thought. "It might be messy in the machine shed." The life of a forensic pathologist is never dull; it goes from calmly quiet to quite busy in the blink of an eye (or the ring of a pager).

The counties I serve are located on the edge of a rapidly growing metropolitan area. As I drove down the county road, I observed all the new homes springing up in what once had been farm fields accustomed to tractors, corn, and soybeans. Many farmers in the area had sold their land to wealthy developers hungry for land. But there were a few who stubbornly resisted the exchanging of money for land or, more importantly, for a way of life.

I slowed down at the wooden sign for Rainbow Farms, a faded rainbow painted above big green letters. Squad cars lined the driveway, and the sheriff's deputy at the end of the driveway checked my ID before allowing me in.

Roger waved to me and walked up as I parked. I saw the crime lab sergeant look over as I pulled in. The training we had done with law enforcement based on the U.S. Department of Justice's guidelines for death scene investigations really paid off, I thought. These people worked together like a well-oiled machine.

My investigator and the sergeant began to fill in the details. A neighbor had stopped by to borrow a saw blade and discovered his friend collapsed in a pool of blood in the shed. He quickly backed out and called 911.

The first officer to arrive at the scene saw a man on the bloody floor. No machinery was running, but several tools and numerous assorted pieces of metal and rubber belts appeared to have been dumped off an overturned bench near the body. The man was dressed in his coveralls. His wallet was still in his back pocket. Blood was on the walls, the bench, and many of the tools.

"Have the photos been taken yet?" I asked.

"Yes," the sergeant replied. "The crime lab team is in there now, processing and documenting a path to the body."

"Roger, do you have any preliminary photos I could see?"

"Yes, right here, Doc," he replied and thrust several into my hand.

"Sergeant, when will I be able to enter the scene and examine the body?" I asked.

"Give us another fifteen minutes, Doc, and we can go in together." He turned and walked briskly back to the machine shed.

WITH A FEW MINUTES TO MYSELF, I began to look around the immediate area. The place had once been quite beautiful, I thought.

I always teach my investigators that a death investigation is really a life investigation: people often die as they live. Keep an open mind, for many times a casual observation yields a clue about a person's dearest thoughts, dreams, or fears.

A death investigation is also the most intimate examination I can imagine. The weathered photograph in a wallet, the contents of a refrigerator or wastebasket, a tattoo, and dirty fingernails all speak volumes to those who care to look.

Investigators realize that everything, from the clothes we wear to the vehicle we drive, the food we eat, the haircut or jewelry we choose, makes a statement. Although most people are not aware of it, virtually every choice begins as a thought.

As I stood in the yard, I observed the neat white house with blue and yellow paint peeling from its shutters. Purple lilies and black-eyed Susans spilled from the garden onto the lawn. The yellow and green parts of a broken lawn mower were strewn across the cement walkway. I stepped over the pieces as I walked up to the kitchen door. The door handle was worn, and the latch didn't quite catch. Flies and mosquitoes were abundant inside.

The walls were the color of tallow, and the lace curtains were tinged brown. The smell of cigarettes clung to the furniture and filled the air. A gray Formica table was surrounded by four chairs, only one of which seemed to be used; its seat cushion was cracked, with foam rubber spilling out. Plates with dried food were piled on the table, and numerous ashtrays were overflowing with cigarette butts. The refrigerator was bare except for beer and pickles, and the freezer was filled with TV dinners.

I ventured cautiously past the sink, piled high with more dirty cups, plates, and silverware, and into the parlor. Thick dust coated a lovely old table and the red velvet seats on the chairs. A buffet contained pretty porcelain dishes, crystal goblets, and lace. Old portraits hung on the wall: couples in starched collars and black overcoats. Eyes pierced mine from across the years. This room smelled different, old and musty, but with a faint hint of perfume.

The bedroom was separated from the parlor by an old curtain hung from a slightly bent metal rod. The four-poster double bed was unmade. Next to the four-drawer chest stood a woman's dainty vanity with a beveled mirror. A hairbrush, hand mirror, and pink container of powder sat primly upon a crocheted doily. A child's crayon drawing of a rainbow was propped against the frame of the vanity mirror.

I glimpsed an old picture frame on the bedside table. The photo showed a young couple in wedding attire. She was beautiful in her gown, with dark brown hair piled high on her head and curls cascading down her back. She proudly clutched a bouquet of flowers, and a handsome man in suit and tie, with a smile on his face, equally proudly held her close. Under the photo were the words ROSE AND HAROLD, JUNE 12, 1946.

Other worn photos were nearby: images of children, ponies, tables of vegetables, celebrations, friends, and family. Without disturbing a thing, I started to see the story of his life: a beautiful love, hard work, children, cigarettes, and dreams.

Just then Roger's voice split the air. "Doc, we are ready for you!" I jumped into action, startled by the sound.

"I'll be right there," I replied.

THE DOORS OF THE MACHINE SHED had been pried off to allow in more light. Tools, belts, half-repaired motors, slats, and coils of wire filled every bit of space on the floor and wall shelves. Mr. Olson's body was face down, fully clothed, and cold. Blood appeared to have been sprayed on the workbench and wall and had pooled on the floor beneath his face and chest.

"When photos are done, let's bag his hands to preserve any evidence," I said. "I don't see any defense injuries on his hands or arms, but there's so much blood. What happened here?" I wondered aloud.

"We didn't see any weapons. There doesn't seem to be any

motive," the sergeant said. "His wallet is still in his back pocket, and his gold watch is on his wrist."

We rolled the body over and looked carefully for injuries. None were apparent but with all that blood, my assessment would have to wait until the autopsy. "Call for transport when the lab is ready," I said.

"Already done, Doc," Roger replied.

"Have you notified next of kin?" I looked at Roger.

"Yes, his daughter has been informed and knows we will be doing a postmortem exam."

"Will you look at him today, Doc?" the sergeant asked eagerly.

"I think I'd better, since you'll have to keep this place secure till we get some answers," I replied.

"I'll send a detective down. What time will you start the exam?"

I glanced at my watch; it was 4 P.M. "Six o'clock. See you then."

ON MY WAY BACK TO THE HOSPITAL, I reflected on the three critical components of a good death investigation: the scene investigation, knowledge of the circumstances, and the autopsy. If any part is missing or incomplete, conclusions about cause or manner of death can be wrong. "Keep an open mind," I thought.

At six o'clock, my assistant and the detective met me at the morgue, and we began the meticulous process of documenting the body of evidence. The goal of the forensic autopsy is to document trauma or disease. The evidence gathered can implicate the actions of another and provide valuable clues to investigators who attempt to solve the mystery. The postmortem examination is regarded as a "power tool" to help correlate the injuries to the death scene and, as always, to determine what really happened.

The cool, bright morgue was a stark contrast to the bloody scene at the farm as we began our work. Photographs, X-rays, trace-evidence collection, and fingernail clippings were followed by body diagrams, dictation, and sketches. Mr. Olson was seventy-three years old, with blue eyes and silver-tinged brown hair. Positive identification was made by comparison with his Minnesota driver's license.

His hands appeared strong and worn; dirt was ground into the folds of his knuckles. I could see and smell the tobacco stains on the index finger and thumb of his right hand. His arms, neck, and face were deeply tanned, and I marveled how his shoulders, arms, and chest were still thickly muscled. He appeared somewhat thin for his size, but I remembered the TV dinners in his freezer and dismissed it.

Surprisingly, and much to my concern, we found no sign of injuries, but profuse bleeding was apparent from the mouth and nose. However, the internal examination began to tell his story.

I made the Y-shaped incision and carefully reflected back the skin, muscle, and connective tissue to expose the organs of the chest and abdominal cavity. I first observed his lungs and heart. The lung tissues were blackened by years of cigarette smoke. Tiny bubbles, or blebs, dotted all the surfaces, changes consistent with emphysema. It was apparent that the left lung was abnormal: the lower lobe was dark purple, congested, and firm to the touch, findings that usually signify pneumonia.

I removed the chest organs, both the heart and lungs,

together and moved them to the dissecting table. As the detective moved closer to observe, I carefully dissected away the esophagus and then began to examine the pulmonary blood vessels and airways. "I found it!" I exclaimed. "I found the source of the blood."

The detective crowded up to the table, looking uncomfortable with the required goggles, mask, and gown. I opened up the blood-filled airways to reveal a large cancerous tumor arising from the left main-stem bronchus, or airway. The tumor was so large that it completely plugged the airway, creating the right conditions for pneumonia in the left lower lobe of lung.

"But why all the blood at the scene, Doc?"

"Look here." I pointed to the edge of the tumor, which had invaded through the bronchus into the aorta. "He bled because the tumor eroded through the wall of the bronchus and punched a hole into the aorta, the large vessel that carries blood from the heart to the rest of the body. Once the tumor pierced the aorta, the blood pressure within the aorta caused massive hemorrhage into the airway. It filled his airways and . . . he would have started to cough, and in the process, blood began to spray all over his machine shed. Once it began, there was no way the bleeding could be stopped and he . . ."

"He bled out?" The detective finished my sentence.

"Yes," I said. "Did you see all the cigarettes and overflowing ashtrays at his house?" He shook his head no.

"Do you see these changes in his lungs?" I asked. "The black color is from the tar, and the bubbly appearance from tissue breakdown and scarring from inhaling all that smoke."

"Well, yeah, I guess so," he answered with disappointment in his voice.

"The death is really due to this man's habits, a lifetime of smoking. He died from exsanguination due to cancer of the lung."

"Wow," he said shaking his head. "When will people ever learn that butts are bad for them? I wish more people could see what I just saw. Those lungs were so black!" He peeled off his gown, adjusted his duty belt, and rinsed off his hands. "I'm outta here, then."

"Tell the captain to release the scene. This death will be classified as natural," I called to him, and he gestured okay.

After everyone had left, I sat down to call Mr. Olson's daughter. She answered with concern in her voice. When I explained the results, she wept. "Thank you so much," she sobbed. "In some ways I am glad he didn't die from injuries, but those cigarettes. We kept telling him to stop! Mom did, too. I wish he had listened."

"I am so sorry." And I added. "Your mom sounds like a wonderful woman."

"Oh, she was. She died four years ago; Dad was lost without her." I heard her take a deep breath. "Now we will have to sell the farm. Mom named it Rainbow Farms because she just loved the song 'Somewhere over the Rainbow' from *The Wizard of Oz.* She always felt her dreams came true there."

I drove home that evening, tired but satisfied that we had solved the case.

I guess I really have learned to trust the process of investigation; make observations, keep an open mind, use all the knowledge you can find, and then . . . trust yourself. It seems to be good advice for life.

WHAT REALLY HAPPENED

M any years of practicing forensic pathology have brought me into many different situations. Usually, I can draw on my education and training to handle them. There have been some situations, however, for which I was never truly prepared, and I was left with the thought, "What *really* happened here, anyway?" The following incident happened while I was practicing forensic pathology in Anoka County, Minnesota, after being appointed coroner in 1993.

Early one winter morning, police officers in my jurisdiction discovered the tracks of a car leading off the roadway, which they followed to find a vehicle overturned into a frozen creek bed. It was 4:45 in the morning, the engine was still running, and the driver was slumped over the wheel with obvious head injuries. Paramedics rushed to the scene and transported the victim, later identified as a twenty-six-year-old, recently married man, to the ER.

The head injuries were extensive, and despite all resuscitative efforts, the man was declared brain dead several hours later. He had been identified through his Minnesota driver's license, and his wife, as legal next of kin, was notified. She rushed to the emergency department to see her husband and never left his side during the following desperate hours as it became apparent that he had suffered irreparable brain injuries and would not survive.

This was at the time when organ and tissue donation was in its infancy. Medical and hospital staffs as well as family members were just becoming aware of the life-giving importance of the gifts of tissue and organ donation. Tissues such as bone, skin, and connective tissue can be donated by family after death. But important organs, such as the heart, lungs, pancreas, and liver, can be harvested and used only when the heart is still beating but the patient has been pronounced "brain dead." This situation does not happen frequently and is the reason that even today these organ donations are scarce.

This patient met the criteria for brain death, but since the death was due to trauma, a coroner's investigation was indicated. The emergency room head nurse notified me and filled in the details. I had to be sure the death investigation was not compromised and, in such cases as this, had to approve the donation of organs. I remember our conversation well, since it was the first time I had ever made that decision.

"Would you allow the donation of organs — a beating

heart, lungs, kidneys, and pancreas — before the autopsy?" the nurse asked. "The family would really like to donate."

"Do there appear to be any injuries to the trunk, chest, or abdomen?"

"No," she answered, "only to the head. But I'll hand the phone over to the surgeon in charge."

A deep but familiar voice came over the line. "How are you, Dr. A? This is Dr. Tom Cook, the ER attending surgeon."

"Hi, Tom. I understand the family would like to donate the organs. Do you see any injury to the chest or abdomen?"

"It appears to be all head injury, Janis. The CT scan showed numerous cranial fractures and extensive intracerebral bleeding [bleeding within the brain], but the chest and abdominal scans were reviewed by the radiologist and read as clear, with no evidence for internal injury."

"Okay, thanks, Tom. Then let the team harvest the chest and abdominal organs. I will perform the autopsy tomorrow to document the head injuries when they are finished."

"Great, thanks so much, Janis! I'll let the family know, too; it'll help them make some sense out of this tragedy."

As I hung up the phone, I felt satisfied. It felt like we all had done the best job possible under such sad circumstances. I notified my investigator of the death so that he could begin gathering the documents and sent him to investigate the scene, where the vehicle had crashed,

I FINISHED MY HOSPITAL DUTIES that day, and as the afternoon slipped into evening, I hurried across the street to my desk in the coroner's office. As I started through the tunnel that connected the hospital and the professional building, I saw the hospital chaplain. Even from a distance he looked concerned. As his eyes met mine, he raised his hand and said, "I have to talk with you about the fatality in the emergency room." I stepped up my pace to meet him in the empty tunnel.

"Everything went well. I spoke with the attending physician and okayed the tissue and organ donation prior to the autopsy," I said.

"I am pleased," he replied, "but that's not what I wanted to tell you."

"What is it, then?"

"I think we had better go back to your office," he said. "You're not going to believe this." The hospital chaplain was a tall, wonderfully pleasant man with a big heart and gentle eyes. He always chose his words carefully and was known for his kindness and compassion. As I unlocked my office door, he asked, "Do you know how the body of this young man was found?"

"Yes," I said, "by the Coon Rapids Police Department in a frozen creek bed at about 4:45 A.M."

"No," he said. "Do you know how they *really* found him?"

"Tell me," I said.

"I spoke with his young wife, who was in the ER with her mother. She said they had just recently been married. He was working an overtime shift to make extra money as a down payment for their house. But then she said something that really stopped me."

"What?" I asked as he paused.

"She told me that she had a dream while she was asleep that

night, a profound dream, in which her husband was standing by her bedside apologizing, telling her that he loved her and that he had been in an accident. His vehicle was in a ditch where it couldn't be seen from the road. She abruptly awoke and realized it was 4:20 in the morning. She called 911 and with absolute certainty told the dispatcher her husband was in an accident not far from their home and that his car was in a ravine where he could not be seen from the road. His body was discovered by officers less than twenty minutes later."

I felt a chill go down my back. "Let me call the police," I said as I reached for the phone. The desk sergeant on duty confirmed with his dispatch the time of the wife's call and its content. "That is amazing!" I said to the chaplain. "Did she say anything else?"

"No," he said thoughtfully, looking down, "except one thing. She told me that it didn't really seem to be a dream. She said he was really standing there, next to her bed."

I completed the postmortem examination the following day after the family generously donated the young man's heart, lungs, kidneys, pancreas, and eyes. The death was classified as an accident and attributed to blunt-force head injuries. I was never able to speak personally with his wife since she was too overcome by her grief and her family had circled protectively around her.

As I pondered my conversation with the chaplain, I also reflected on the advice I had from Cal Bandt and that I now so often pass on: gather information, make observations, and most importantly, don't rush to judgment; *trust* that you will arrive at the truth.

There was no doubt in my heart that our conversation, shared that late afternoon in my office, felt like the truth about what really happened. But it was not something that could be proved as a medical certainty. It was simply there, and its presence seemed more a gentle reminder than a challenge.

PART III

THE SECOND SECRET
WE ALREADY KNOW THIS

All learning is remembering. A good teacher causes
students to remember what they already know.

— NEALE DONALD WALSCH

HOW COULD I
HAVE FORGOTTEN?

Experiences of life after death have been told and retold thousands of times over many centuries in virtually all religions and cultures. But the *recognition* of these experiences to which I am referring is different from a "teaching" or lesson. For many, the retelling of a modern-day account of a dream, visit, or synchronicity elicits tears of joy at the reconnection or sometimes a deep and comfortable "aha!" It seems to be part of our cellular memory, an innate knowing that reorders our thoughts and awareness. Let me explain.

One day, while lecturing at a forensic seminar, just before the morning break I brought up these extraordinary experiences and mentioned my observations of their profound effects. As I made my way out of the auditorium, a woman came up to my side. She seemed intent on catching my attention.

"Doctor, I work with a health care organization in the area.

I learned a lot from your lecture, all except for the last part." I paused with a bit of concern. She glanced at the floor. "That last part about those 'experiences' feels…so familiar! Like I knew it once but forgot it. I'm anxious to remember it again. Tell me, how could I have forgotten?" she said intently. I felt both relieved and surprised.

"I've asked myself the same question," I replied. "I don't know the answer, but maybe it is no coincidence we are all remembering together."

I have found that many people have an overwhelming sense of recognition when these extraordinary experiences are told or retold, written or rewritten. It is almost as though the listener can finish the experience by heart, just by imagining the most-hoped-for, the grandest possibility. I often tell my audiences, "You don't need to purchase my book or listen to this lecture. You already know all of this!" Recognition is only the first part, as Dr. Bandt taught me. Then you must trust your own feelings, intuition, and perceptions; in other words, *trust* that you will know the truth.

What would the world be like if we chose to really "know what we know"? Perhaps we would become more deliberate and thoughtful; and we might begin to wonder who we really are.

I suspect that we would begin to treat ourselves and others with great reverence. I suspect we might even treat the earth and its creatures with care. I suspect all who read these words will know in their own hearts exactly what that would mean. And, of course, that would change everything.

What an extraordinary thought, to trust that we already *know* all of this.

SUSAN AND GRANDPA DEWITT

Look and you will find it.
What is unsought will be undetected.

— SOPHOCLES

My husband, a police officer, was asked to be the best man at his friend Ryan Law's wedding to Sara. It was a clear, sun-drenched, very hot July day. The church was beautifully decorated, spacious and cool. So many friends in law enforcement attended. At the ceremony the priest commented on just how well protected he felt in both a heavenly and earthly sense, and that it seemed no coincidence the groom's surname was Law.

Ryan was serving in the Hennepin County sheriff's office as a jailor and, when off duty, was a death investigator for Anoka County. Sara, his charming, athletic, and energetic bride, taught fourth grade at a local elementary school.

The reception was held at a well-worn VFW hall in the neighborhood. Strings of twinkling lights, folding chairs, long tables, and familiar music reminded me of Italian weddings I had attended as a child in my father's hometown, Duluth. It was there I first learned how to dance, and especially to polka, from my older cousins, uncles, and friends. This wedding seemed no different.

After the customary photos and receiving line, white-clad waiters brought out bowls and platters of fruit salad, fresh buns, mashed potatoes with gravy, buttered green beans, and steaming, tender roast beef. With my husband and his friends already seated at the head table, I found myself pleasantly mingling with their friends and family members as I went through the serving line, balancing my plate, silverware, glass, and napkin.

A petite, smart-looking young woman with a pretty black dress, dancing blue eyes, and long brown hair came up to me as I searched among the long tables for a place to sit. "You're Dr. A, aren't you? Tom's wife?"

"Yes, I am Tom's wife, and you are...?"

"Susan. I am a friend of Ryan's. We work together at the jail. You know, I don't know anybody else here. Can I sit with you?"

"Of course you can. I'd love to sit with you," I said as we spotted two chairs at the end of a table near the side of the hall.

We settled onto the metal chairs, and I quickly grabbed my napkin and silverware, suddenly aware of how hungry I felt. The plate of food looked very inviting. "How did you meet Ryan?" I asked casually.

"We started at the jail together. I usually work in the intake area, booking the prisoners as they come in." And then she said quite directly, "I want you to know something, Dr. A. I read your book. Ryan gave it to me. It's changed my life. It has truly changed my life."

I remember being surprised — and curious — at her direct-ness and obvious candor as I dug into the mashed potatoes and gravy. "Susan, how did reading the book change your life?"

She looked at me, then glanced down. "I really can't put it into words, but if I did, I would say I'm more aware of things, things I didn't understand before." She hesitated a moment, and I thought that perhaps I should change the subject. After all, I barely knew her; I thought perhaps I shouldn't have asked.

But then she began again, with a more confident tone. "Dr. Amatuzio, I'd like to tell you something. After I read your book, I had a dream. Since all my grandparents have died, I basically adopted my best friend's grandpa for my own. His name is Dewitt, Grandpa Dewitt. We have always had a spe-cial connection. Up until early last summer he lived in a nurs-ing home in New Brighton. He had severe lung disease and was on oxygen. When I would visit, I would carry the oxygen tank (it was heavy!) and follow him around. I think sometimes we looked a little funny because he would grin slyly and joke to his buddies, 'Look who I just picked up!'

"But we had such good times, and we had such good talks about life, and things, you know." I nodded, remembering my own grandfathers. "I just loved his little ways," she added, "even the way he smelled like old shirts, suspenders, and Old Spice aftershave.

"Last summer he had to move to a different nursing home, but this one had lovely grounds. There was a pond with a foun-tain in the middle of it and plenty of flowers. He often asked me to visit so we could go down and sit by the fountain and look at the flowers. He said it was his favorite spot." She glanced down softly and added, "But I didn't get there last summer. I had just started my new job at the sheriff's office, and I just didn't make the time. But I was determined to go visit him this summer.

"Two nights after I read your book, I had a dream; Grandpa Dewitt came to visit me. He looked wonderful, and he was so happy. He took me by the hand and we went down to the pond with the fountain in it. We sat there and had the best talk ever, about all sorts of things. I remember being *so* incredibly happy. It was just wonderful. In fact, when I awakened, I felt we had actually talked, it was so vivid; I felt like he had really been there.

"I decided to call him right then, that morning, and go with him to see that pond and fountain for myself. As I reached for the phone, well, you know what happened, don't you? It rang! I was even more startled when I heard my girlfriend's voice on the line. 'Susan,' she said in a tearful voice, 'I got a call from the nursing home this morning, just now. Grandpa Dewitt died last night! They found him in bed; they said he just died in his sleep!'"

"Oh, my," I said. "Really!"

"Yes," Susan nodded, her eyes brimming with tears, her meal virtually untouched. She looked down, dropped her fork. "I have to go now," she said, unable to hold back the tears. "Thank you for listening."

I finished my meal in silence. Some things still never fail to surprise me. What really happened? Was it just an unusual coincidence? Or perhaps Susan remembered something she had forgotten; her awareness shifted and expanded.

And Grandpa Dewitt stopped by to visit, and talk, and reassure her that he was fine ... and so was she.

MATT'S BUCK

It is only with the heart one sees rightly;
that which is essential is invisible to the eye.

— ANTOINE DE SAINT-EXUPÉRY, *THE LITTLE PRINCE*

I teach classes for law enforcement and death investigators on a variety of forensic subjects. The classes are designed to help those who investigate the circumstances and scenes of death understand better the variety of situations encountered and the details that must be gathered. These investigations are really about teamwork. The professionals, both law enforcement and medico-legal death investigators, are the forensic pathologist's eyes and ears at the scene, helping shape the questions that must be answered in the autopsy suite and toxicology laboratory in order to speak for the dead.

The other reason I teach, and perhaps the more important one to me, is to get to know the team of people who share this job with me. In order to "speak for the dead," to reveal what *really* happened, many eyes and many perspectives are needed.

In class we begin to talk to one another, and during and after class we often eat together and sometimes even laugh and joke together. When classes extend over a period of time, relationships are forged and friendships are made. And then I am confident that any investigative problem or unusual forensic situation can be solved through the process of caring, collaboration, and collective wisdom of the group. These relationships are the foundations of success.

One evening during a class break, a deputy sheriff named Matt came up to talk to me and asked if I could bring a copy of my book *Forever Ours* for him the next time we met for class. I did as he asked, and as the class progressed over its five Monday evenings, he came up frequently to talk. I appreciated his questions and comments.

One evening he said, "You know, Doc, I liked your book; the stories were great, but I would like to know something. Why doesn't everyone have these experiences?"

"That's a good question. I don't know the answer."

"How can I get one?" he asked, looking intently. I paused and looked at him. He was so diligent and insistent.

"Who died? Who are you missing?" I said gently.

"My father." He looked down quickly, his eyes filling with tears. "My dad died ten years ago, and I don't feel like he has ever contacted me." The small classroom was bustling with noise, and people milled around us.

"You know, Matt, I have a feeling that our loved ones stop at nothing to let us know that they are perfectly fine. I think they let us know in every way possible. Perhaps we just don't recognize it."

He looked thoughtful and said, "I'll think about that. Thanks!"

The next time our class met, Matt came up at the break to talk. "You know, Doc, if anyone was going to come back, it would have been my dad. I guess I have been looking for a concrete message, not something I'd have to figure out. But while I've been thinking about this, I remembered something.

"My dad and I hunted together every season since I can remember. With deer hunting season coming up in a few short weeks, I guess I have been feeling sad because I have been missing him — and his brother, my Uncle Lavern. I remembered the first season after Dad's death. It was pretty difficult for me; I was in his stand, using his favorite rifle, and feeling pretty lonely.

"Dad built his stand next to a marsh on the property where he was born. It was his favorite place in the world, and it is where we loved to hunt together. The stand has a beautiful view, and he would be there all day, every day of hunting season, whether he saw a deer or not. One time before he had his heart attack, he and I were up on the stand, and he pointed to an opening across the marshy pond. 'I built this stand here because some day a big buck is going to come across the marsh, right through that opening,' he said confidently, pointing to a break in the trees across the marsh. But it never happened for him.

"On my first day of hunting opener without him, I was out early in the morning. I climbed into his stand before dawn and hunkered down. I was really missing him and couldn't think of much else. As the sun came up, I looked to my right and saw a big buck coming my way. I could have shot, but I didn't. He disappeared behind some brush and then suddenly bolted in front of my stand and ran way out into the marsh in front of me and disappeared as quickly as he had appeared. I waited and blamed myself for missing my chance.

"Then I glanced across the marsh, to the exact spot where my dad always hoped he'd see a deer. And there in the clearing stood the buck looking at me. There was no reason, I thought, for him to come back out of the brush except of course to give me this message."

He looked down and paused. "I know Dad was letting me know he was right there, letting me know that everything was just fine and that he was watching. Every season now, for ten years in a row since his death, I've gone out to the stand, but I have *never* seen a buck right in that particular spot again. So I think you are right. Our loved ones *are* always with us, and they stop at nothing to let us know how much they care."

"Thanks, Matt," I said and smiled to myself. Then I walked to the front of the class to resume my lecture.

Five years have passed since Matt shared his story with me; he is retired from law enforcement now. When I contacted him about using his experience in this book he shared with me one more gift, written on the last day of deer season, 2005:

Why does deer season still cause me such problems? I think I have it figured out.

Hunting is just hunting to me, but deer season is different. Nine days in November make me anxious and still bring with them loneliness. It isn't even the feeling of being alone or far from home. It's the loneliness for people, places, and times that no longer exist, except in my mind.

During deer season the fabric of time is thin. The past is so close you can almost touch it. It feels as if you could see through it if you could just find the right spot. Sometimes I try, but I haven't found it yet. It feels as if something is tugging me by the heart and trying to pull me through, but I can't go.

I notice the light in the forest is different during deer season. It is softer, as if being filtered through cheese-cloth. It is different than any other time of year. As if it was coming from somewhere else.

I know my dad, Hartvick, and my uncle Lavern are there, just out of sight. Maybe they can see me. Maybe others are there too.

When I close my eyes, I can see Dad and Lavern coming out of the misty forests of time on opening morning, wearing their red coats and carrying their rifles. Not with my eyes, even though I try real hard, but in my head, and in my heart. They are young and strong and happy to help us get what we need for the winter. Some-times I can feel their easy humor and almost hear them laugh and joke; I think they do their best to help me, especially when I mess up or miss my shot.

The last day of deer season is hard. On this day I close my eyes and see Dad and Laverne walking back to wherever it is, vanishing into the softly lit woods. They turn and look back, then disappear; like in a dream. Gone till I return once more, next season.

BUDDY

Doctor, have you ever heard a story about a dog?" And before I could reply the woman said, "I have one for you. His name was Buddy."

I had just finished speaking to a most wonderful group of people, all hospital volunteers. These are the great folks who staff the gift shop, the surgical waiting room, and the coffee shop and who assist patients leaving the hospital following surgery or a short hospital stay. This group of mostly elders was finishing a two-day seminar for hospital auxiliary members at a lakeside resort in northern Minnesota. My lecture was the last one of the day, to be followed by lunch. When the audience members stood up following my presentation, I assumed they were heading for their meal; instead, they gave me a standing ovation! I was both happily surprised and a little bewildered at their outpouring of support. As the applause subsided, a pleasant, confident-looking woman approached with the question, "Have you ever heard a story about a dog?" So we simply sat down together on the podium stage, and she told me her story.

"My husband loves to hunt so he purchased a black Labrador puppy; we named him Buddy." A smile spilled over her face. "Sometimes we choose our pets, but most times, I really think they choose us. Buddy became *my* dog, and my steadfast companion and friend. Despite several tries on my husband's part, it seemed that Buddy didn't really like to hunt. I didn't mind when my husband left, but I just couldn't bear to have Buddy gone, too, so we always spent hunting season at home together when my husband was off in the wild.

"When Buddy was about three years old, he began to lose weight. We couldn't figure out why, so I took him to the vet, where he was diagnosed with Crohn's disease. Well, I guess you know that this disease causes inflammation of the small intestine so it can't really absorb your food and you lose weight. But Buddy was treated with medication and began to improve, much to our joy.

"At about this time my husband's mother fell and broke her hip. She recovered well in the hospital but was reluctant to go to a nursing home. We offered to have her recuperate at our home instead. This arrangement pleased all of us, in particular Buddy. Unknown to us, Grandma was not particularly fond of dogs and especially not ones that love to play fetch all day. But that little Labrador had other ideas; he slowly worked his magic on her, and they became fast friends, even though Grandma wouldn't let on how much she liked Buddy.

"Grandma was recuperating well, and we began to notice that she would get up to use the bathroom every night about midnight. She always slept with her door closed, but when she got up at that hour of the night, Buddy had a habit of sneaking into her bedroom and jumping into the warm spot on her bed. When she would return, she would just push him over, and the two would sleep peacefully tucked together in bed until the following morning, when she would shoo him out, thinking that nobody would notice. I figured it out with all those black hairs in her bed! This routine continued, and we all played along. When she was well, Grandma decided to return to her condominium in Florida to be with other family members and friends. We missed her but were pleased that she could go back to her home.

"Over the next several months Buddy began to lose weight again. A visit to the vet revealed his condition had worsened — the medications were no longer working. After several months of desperate struggles and special diets, Buddy was still not thriving, and we decided to put him down. Our good-byes were tearful; he really was one of the family.

"We did not have the heart to tell Grandma what happened during our weekly call two days later. But then she said, 'A couple of nights ago I had the strangest thing happen to me. I got up at midnight to go to the bathroom. When I returned to bed, Buddy was sitting by the side of my bed. I saw him jump right up into my warm spot. So I pushed him over like always, and we slept together for the rest of night.'

"Then I told her what had happened, that we had put Buddy down two days earlier. Grandma was deeply saddened and said how much she would miss her little friend." By now this lovely lady seated next to me had tears streaming down her cheeks.

Then she put her face in her hands and wept. "I miss him."

I put my arm around her shoulder and said, "Thank you. Thank you so much." Several others had gathered around and had listened thoughtfully. Some were dabbing their eyes, smiling and nodding.

My mother says, "Growing old is for the brave." I think I'm beginning to understand what she means. As we grow old, we so often lose loved ones and friends. My grandmother used to say, "They are all up on the hill now; all but me!"

Aging adds immediacy to the reality that life is filled with loss, and as we age, we may choose to see more clearly, both outwardly and within. We may spend more time in the space of our thoughts. Hopefully, we will realize their power and know we are never alone.

Many before us have shown the way, shown there is nothing to fear, and all is well. As we grow old we can choose to act on what we already know, with wisdom, and love, and grace.

In the words of Elizabeth Barrett Browning, "Grow old along with me; the best is yet to be."

PART IV

THE THIRD SECRET
WE ARE AWAKENING

The starting point of consciousness is awe.

— KIRK SCHNEIDER, *AWE-BASED LEARNING*

WE ARE AWAKENING

I have begun to think that our fascination with all things forensic, reflected in the media with television shows such as *CSI*, *Crossing Jordan*, *Law and Order*, and others, may signify an important milestone in our level of awareness. Events surrounding a death, especially an unusual one, are fascinating of course, and so is the process of making the discovery of "what really happened." Death investigators and forensic pathologists alike are glorified; some achieve a movie star–like status almost overnight. The term *forensic* is ubiquitous, and many young people, thrilled and enthralled by the excitement of "solving the crime," seek a career in this field. And yet, again, perhaps this fascination is also a metaphor for a shift in the level of our consciousness.

In any death investigation, the crucial responsibility is to speak for the dead. Through the investigation of the death scene and other situations, the gathering of the medical and social history, and the autopsy, the story unfolds to answer the question "What happened?" The other and equally important task is making a positive identification, in other words, answering the question "Who are you?" Then family members can be notified, property distributed, and funeral arrangements made. The finest investigators I know use their education and training as well as their street smarts and common sense. More basically put, they trust their instincts. Instinct, or intuition, is honed by experience, much as wisdom is tempered by knowledge. Intuition works when we pay attention to it.

The process of death investigation shifted for me to reveal larger truths when I started looking at it from a slightly different perspective, through the lens of wonder. The questions become not "Who are you?" but "Who are we?" Not "What happened?" but "What happens?"

Perhaps we have to combine the power of precise forensic observation with the strength of our intuition and awe. It seems that when objective, dispassionate observations are enhanced with internal recognition or knowing, passion and excitement emerge, wisdom awakens, and a deeper vision of life emerges.

In the context of the familiar "extraordinary" experiences retold on these pages, the answers I sought unfolded. I became thrilled and excited at the riveting possibility that these stories were indeed true. Both wonder and humility filled my heart as I realized the incredible beauty of the web of life.

Albert Einstein wrote, "Thoughts influence the body." For

a moment, dare to think as Einstein did. Sense the excitement, joy, and hope that are palpable when the imagination soars to the grandest of possibilities about "who we are" and "what happens." With the retelling of these extraordinarily *common* experiences, the answers become apparent. Could they really be true?

The answer, my friend, is found within. And of course, that changes everything.

MY DONOR'S NAME IS DANNE

Kim sat anxiously in the surgical waiting room at Latter Day Saints Hospital in Salt Lake City, Utah, in the spring of 1994. Her sister was asleep in the chair next to her. The long-awaited phone call from the transplant coordinator had come last evening. "We have a match!" the coordinator excitedly told her. "We have both a kidney and a pancreas for your husband. Please come to the hospital right away."

Kim and Mike had waited a long time for this day. Mike had been diagnosed with insulin-dependent diabetes mellitus as a child. Now he was thirty-two years old with a wife and three children. He had carefully controlled his blood sugars over the years with multiple daily insulin injections. However, despite his attention, the disease continued to take its toll on his kidneys, blood vessels, eyes, and nerves. Mike's physician,

Dr. Harry Laughton, a well-known endocrinologist, had urged Mike to consider a pancreas and kidney transplant, although at that time this was still considered an experimental treatment. Only three others had been performed at Latter Day Saints Hospital. Mike treasured life and desperately wanted to be there to see his children grow up. He jumped at the opportunity and began the rigorous testing and preparation for the transplant.

Mike had been in surgery for over six hours. Kim was dozing in the family room between frequent updates from the operating room staff. Now one of the aides notified her that the physician would be in to speak with her soon; the procedure had gone well, and the surgical team was closing. Shortly thereafter, the chief surgeon walked in, a smile on his face. "We did it, and Mike is doing well," he said. "We're not out of the woods yet, but now he has a chance at a full life."

"When can I see him?" Kim asked.

"At least another hour, as soon as we've stabilized him in the post-anesthesia recovery room and he's awake. Why don't you get something to eat and come back in a little while," the surgeon suggested.

The time passed quickly for Kim, and the door opened once again. "You can come in now," a nurse from the recovery room said. "He is just arousing from the anesthesia." Kim walked through the doors. Tears welled up in her eyes as she saw her husband. An aide put a chair next to the bed and pulled the curtains partway to give them some privacy. Kim leaned forward and kissed her husband lightly on the cheek, her hand cupped gently over his. "Mike, I am here," she whispered. He turned his head toward her touch and opened his eyes.

"Kim." He whispered hoarsely. She bent closer to him. "Kim," he said, "my donor's name is Danne." He smiled faintly and closed his eyes again. Kim slowly sank back in the chair, a puzzled look on her face. She shook her head and then tucked the words away, wondering if they were due to the effects of anesthesia. When she returned to the waiting room, Kim told her sister of Mike's condition and of his cryptic message. Her sister sat up abruptly. "Oh, my gosh, Kim!" she said with alarm. "A man with that name died last night. His name, Danne Lynch, was on the board in the surgical waiting room. Do you think—?"

THIRTY-SIX HOURS EARLIER in New Brighton, Minnesota, Patti Harvey had been awakened from sleep at 3:30 A.M. by the insistent ring of her phone. She sat up in bed and in the instant before she picked it up, she knew it concerned her oldest son.

"Is this Danne Lynch's mother?" the voice on the line asked.

"Yes, it is. This is Patti Harvey."

"This is Dr. Adams from Latter Day Saints Emergency Room in Salt Lake City. Ma'am, your son was severely injured in a car accident this evening," he informed her.

"Is he going to make it?" she asked.

Dr. Adams hesitated.

"I have to know," Patti Harvey said.

"I don't think so," Dr. Adams answered gently. "He is still alive but has very serious head injuries."

"I'll catch the first plane to Salt Lake City. Dr. Adams, please do your best. But no matter what happens, I want you to know my son is an organ donor."

Patti hastily made arrangements to fly to Salt Lake City and in the meantime called hourly for updates. Danne was her oldest son, now twenty-seven, and he had always been a risk taker. He had moved to Salt Lake City eight months earlier, pursuing both a love and a job. On a rainy night, under the influence of alcohol, he had lost control of his car and overturned on a slippery bridge over the Jordan River. His seatbelted passenger walked away from the crash with minor injuries. Danne, who was unrestrained, suffered head injuries that would prove fatal.

The hours after Dr. Adams's phone call passed in a blur for Patti. Friends and family gathered upon hearing the news. Northwest Airlines even held a flight for them, and the family was taken out to board the plane on the runway. When Patti arrived at the hospital in Salt Lake City and saw her son hooked to tubes and a respirator, she knew in her heart that he would not live, but she had the opportunity to spend time at his side during his last hours, grateful that she was there to still care for him.

She recalled one of their last conversations several weeks earlier and how she had almost dismissed it. Danne had just renewed his driver's license and informed her that he had chosen to be an organ donor.

When Danne was pronounced brain dead, the family left the hospital. All the necessary forms for the donor coordinator had been signed. After the transplant procedure was complete, Danne's body was cremated according to his family's wishes, and his remains were sent home for a funeral service in New Brighton.

MIKE RECOVERED STEADILY, although he had to spend the next few days in the intensive care unit, followed by several weeks on the transplant floor where he was monitored for signs of infection or organ rejection. The new kidney and pancreas were working well, and Mike was filled with gratitude and joy.

One afternoon several days after the surgery found Kim sitting and reading in his room. She looked at him and quietly said, "Mike, you said something to me right after surgery. Do you remember?"

"How could I forget?" he answered. "I said 'My donor's name is Danne.' You know, Kim, I saw him . . ."

"How do you know that?" she asked.

"Well, it was the most amazing thing that has ever happened to me, and words don't really explain it."

"Tell me."

"I remember that everything before the operation was a blur. I was so excited and rushed and, you know how I felt —" He paused. "You know, someone died so I can live. That's giving the ultimate gift." And his eyes welled up with tears. "Something happened to me in there. Something *happened* during surgery. At some point I realized I could hear all of the conversations in the operating room, and then I could see what was happening to me from up above. There was no pain; I just watched everything. I saw the organs brought into the OR after mine had been removed. They were in a blue container and packed in ice. At that moment, I felt such an extraordinary wave of love and gratitude. It was so intimate, so profound, that in that moment I said, 'I want to see my donor.'

"In the next instant, I just seemed to pass through a wall. Just like that! And then I saw him; he was lying there. He was a real good-looking man, with long, sandy hair, and he looked about my age. He was thin and, you know, long. The next thing that happened to me — well, again, it's hard to explain."

"I'm listening," she said, fascinated.

Mike paused as if struggling for words. "I was just sucked up into the light. You know, Kim, it was like a giant vacuum cleaner," he said with a smile. "I felt myself suddenly, abruptly lifted up by this incredible force, this light, and I heard the words, 'Danne died and you are going to live.' I saw three luminous beings. One of them I recognized as my aunt. She was wearing the scarf I'd given her before she died. Next to her was Danne, and the other being, well, he was so familiar, someone who had known me all my life, but I just couldn't figure out who he was. I felt such love, such passion, and such joy. Kim, there just aren't words. There aren't words for it." He paused. "But you know, I'm different now. I know something. I *know* who I am, and I will forever know that I was in a sacred, familiar place. I will never fear anything again. Life and love is all there is."

The tears that had begun flowing when he started to tell his story had wet his face and the sheets. "I'm overwhelmed. I have Danne's kidney and pancreas. I am part of Danne's life, and he is part of mine. It was somehow, some way, perfect."

As she listened, Kim suddenly realized that tears had started streaming down her face, too, and they had not stopped the whole time Mike was speaking. "We are blessed," she whispered.

"More than we know," Mike replied.

Mike was released from Latter Day Saints Hospital approximately four weeks later, and he grew stronger with each passing day.

SHORTLY AFTER SHE HAD HEARD her husband's extraordinary story, Kim looked through the obituaries in the local paper. There she found "Danne Lynch, 27-year-old man, died April 15, 1994; survived by his mother and stepfather, Mr. and Mrs. William Harvey, of New Brighton, Minnesota, and father, Robert Lynch, of Ramsey, Minnesota."

Taking an enormous leap of faith, Kim decided to contact the family. She discovered there were three William Harveys listed in New Brighton, Minnesota, and got their phone numbers. She called the first two on her list, but neither recognized the name Danne Lynch. Then, on a hunch, Kim tried something that under normal circumstances would never work. She called 411 again and explained about her husband, his experience, and her mission, and convinced the operator to give her the third William Harvey's address. Several days later, Patti Harvey received a letter in the mail from Kim.

It began, "Dear Mrs. Harvey, You don't know me, but a part of you is very close to me." and concluded "I do not wish to intrude, but if you would like to call, here's our phone number."

PATTI HARVEY, whom I had come to know through a mutual friend, the radio talk show host Brad Walton (Brad had interviewed me about my first book), related this story to me as we had lunch together. "What did you do?" I asked her.

"Well, I called her that very day, in fact, the very instant I read the letter. It felt right to me, and I missed Danne so much!

"Right then and there, I agreed I would meet them several weeks later when I returned to Salt Lake City for another visit. Danne's girlfriend picked me up at the airport, and we drove to Kim and Mike's house. My heart was truly in shreds, and I wasn't sure what to expect. I walked into their home and first met their children. And then I met Mike. His eyes were filled with tears, and he took me in his arms and hugged me for a long time. We sat down in the living room. Their youngest son promptly curled up in my lap and fell asleep.

"I handed Mike a photo of Danne, and he gasped, 'That's him. That's the man I saw.' He then told me of his extraordinary journey on that night of April 15, 1994. I listened in awe, and my heart leaped with joy. When he finished, I put my hand on his little son's head as he slept in my lap. I realized at that moment that my heart was beginning to heal. Michael's experience was for me the gift of life itself."

I put down my pen and sat there amazed.

"There's one more thing, Janis," Patti said. "It's been quite a few years now since Danne died, and Mike and Kim just had their first grandchild. As the years have passed, the donation of my son's organs has given me such a sense of comfort and peace. It has connected me deeply with the beautiful knowing that 'Life goes on.'"

JAMES'S PLAYGROUND

I established the Anoka County Coroner's Office in 1993, while I was still dividing my time between forensic and hospital pathology at Mercy Hospital in Coon Rapids, Minnesota. Because of my work, it was important to me that the coroner's office be located close to the hospital laboratory. Fortunately, I found a small space in the basement of the adjacent doctors' office building, which is conveniently connected to the hospital by a tunnel. My office is still located there. Although cramped and crowded, this office is the place where every morning the investigators and physicians sit down together and review the day's work. We discuss each death investigation and autopsy decision and decide on the necessary follow-up information and phone calls. Our investigative area is arranged around a short peninsula in the back of the office, close to the coffeepot, the old files, the refrigerator, and the coffee cups.

On one particular morning, I remember, I bypassed the investigative desk for a truly needed hot cup of coffee. As I poured the steaming brew into a cup, Bob Kammer, my long-time office investigator, said, "Doc, I think you're going to want to hear about this one."

"Okay," I said, sitting down with anticipation.

Bob told me that Chuck, another veteran death investigator, had been called to investigate the death of a fifteen-year-old boy with muscular dystrophy the night before. "The boy, whose name was James, wasn't registered in hospice yet, although his death was expected," he said. Ordinarily, investigations into the deaths of persons who die at home in a hospice program can be handled over the phone. But since this boy wasn't registered, Chuck had had to make a scene visit.

"James had been in a wheelchair until just recently, when he became too weak to sit up. He had been mainly confined to bed for the last several weeks. His mother reported that just before he died, her son looked up and asked her about the playground and all the children he could see, running and playing."

I felt a smile spread across my face, knowing something extraordinary had happened. "Thanks so much, Bob."

"There's something else, Doc. The mom had a copy of your book, *Forever Ours*; she said you might be interested in talking with her."

SEVERAL WEEKS LATER James's mother, Susan, sat across from me at a restaurant. She had graciously agreed to meet me and tell me about her extraordinary son. "He was three years old when doctors made the diagnosis of muscular dystrophy," she said. "James was our youngest; he had one older brother and two sisters, all strong and healthy. But we knew something was wrong when he kept falling. I had an inkling, a sense that something was wrong because, you see, my own brother had muscular dystrophy, and I remembered his symptoms when he was a little boy."

Progressive muscular dystrophy, or Duchenne muscular dystrophy, as it is technically labeled, is what is called a sex-linked recessive condition — a genetic disease — that virtually always afflicts only boys. Let me explain. Humans have forty-six chromosomes in each nucleated cell. They inherit half from their mothers and half from their fathers. These chromosomes, which contain all of our genes, form twenty-three pairs. Twenty-two of the pairs, or forty-four of the total chromosomes, are called "autosomes": they contain matching types of information, and one member of each pair is received from the father, the other from the mother.

The twenty-third pair is called the "sex chromosomes," and these may or may not "match, depending on the gender of the person. In females this pair does match and is given an XX designation; in males, the pair differs and has an XY designation. What happens is that females receive an X sex chromosome from each parent, while males receive an X sex chromosome from their mothers (the only possibility) and a Y from their fathers. (This is why there is an approximately 50-50 possibility of having a girl or a boy with any pregnancy.)

The abnormal gene for muscular dystrophy is carried on the X sex chromosome of the mother, and the disease only becomes clinically apparent when an abnormal X chromosome is paired with a Y chromosome. When the disease is carried by the mother, she has no symptoms because she also has a normal X chromosome to provide the needed genetic information.

In almost all circumstances, the disease manifests only in sons of mothers who are carriers. These boys have inherited a Y chromosome from their fathers and have a 50 percent chance of inheriting the abnormal X chromosome from their mothers. Boys with this disease become progressively physically debilitated, and James was no exception — except for the fact that he was surprisingly happy and cheerful, and quite sociable.

By six years of age, James was falling so often that his parents got him a wheelchair. He would push himself around the house and neighborhood, often stopping by friends' houses in the neighborhood, uninvited but always welcome. By age eight, he required an electric wheelchair to get around and was delighted at his newfound freedom. His favorite place was always the playground, and he would beg his mom to take him there. Although he couldn't climb, he would spend hours gliding on the swing, and his mom was always with him.

His twelfth year on earth was the best time of his life. He was full of energy and life that shone in his hazel eyes, which were fringed with long eyelashes. He never missed an opportunity to feed birds and squirrels, and he loved to go to Lake Superior in Duluth to watch the water and feed the seagulls that would hover around him.

He stayed in school three more years but became less engaged as his body failed him. Three months before he died, his throat muscles weakened and he became frightened as swallowing and breathing became more difficult. His parents took him out of school right after Christmas.

His mom, Susan, was his primary caregiver and stayed by his side every moment she could. He was content to stay in bed but often asked to be turned from one side to another. One day during that time he asked Susan, "Am I going to die?"

"Yes, you will, James, and so will all of us."

James paused and said, "What is it like to die, Mom?"

Susan's eyes welled up with tears as she related her story. "I searched my heart for the right answer, and said, 'James, it's the most natural thing you could imagine; you just close your eyes and fall asleep and wake up somewhere else.'"

He nodded and smiled. "OK, Mom, I get it! I'm not afraid."

THE DEMANDS OF JAMES'S ILLNESS were taking their toll on him and his family, and all were growing weary. Although Susan had hoped for one more summer for him, she remembers whispering a prayer the night before his death. She prayed, "Lord, we just can't go on any longer. I give him to you. He's your boy now."

At 3 A.M. that night, James called out to his mom again. She hurried to his bedside, and what he said astonished her.

"Mom, will you hold me? I need more gravity!"

"More gravity?!"

"Yes, Mom, more gravity. I am going up."

Susan gently lay down beside him. "Son, I can't give you more gravity."

With that, James called out for his father, "Dad, I need more gravity!"

Susan wrapped her arms around him and said, "Your dad can't give you more gravity either." She hugged and kissed her son and held him tight until he was calm.

After a short while, James stirred again. His eyes were closed tightly when he said to his mom, "What's this playground and all the kids?"

"What playground?" Susan asked as she turned him over toward her.

"That playground, the one with all the kids running and playing!" he responded, looking at her as she asked.

"Do you want me to hold you again?"

"Yes," he answered quietly. Susan gathered him up in her arms and moved to the rocking chair next to the bed. She started to sing one of his favorite songs, "Jesus Loves Me."

"When I got to the verse, 'If I love him when I die, Heaven's gates will open wide,'" Susan told me, "I lifted my hand up toward heaven and said, 'You can take him now' and kissed his cheek, and then he was gone. Through my tears, I looked up and waved, and said, 'Good-bye, sweetheart!'"

A few moments passed, and I realized my eyes had, too, filled with tears. What an extraordinary experience Susan and her beloved son had shared with me. What a vision, I thought, as in my mind's eye I saw James running and skipping wildly with joy and abandon, greeting all his friends.

HIS FAVORITE FIELD

Orval and JoAnn are the salt of the earth, and they happen to be my neighbors and friends. Their farm is one of the oldest operating dairies in Anoka County. Orval's grandfather settled the land in the late 1800s, and his fields stretch over many acres. I became their neighbor when I built a home in Anoka County, near my current practice. Orval is made of the stuff of legends; he is small and strong, steady and determined. Their sons have settled near them, and Orval and JoAnn's home is now filled with grandchildren of many ages.

JoAnn welcomes you into their home and in no time has a plate of fresh cookies or a piece of pie and a hot cup of coffee on the table. One December evening when I was sitting with them at their kitchen table, JoAnn looked at me and said, "A friend of mine, LeAnn, passed away last week. I think her death was reported to your office." She told me the full name, and I nodded. She added, "You must have known, then, that LeAnn had a bit of dementia and wandered outside in the middle of the night into the snow. Her daughter found her out there the next morning. She told me she thought her mom froze to death!"

Indeed, our office had investigated the death of an elderly woman who had wandered out of her home and died from exposure. She had a history of Alzheimer's dementia, a condition which causes confusion and memory loss. "Did you know that last week LeAnn told her daughter that LeAnn's own sister, Wilma, who had died several years earlier was coming to take her home?" I shook my head with a smile, and JoAnn continued, "I haven't often believed in all the things you've written about, but I'd like to tell you about something that happened to me."

She poured me another cup of coffee and began her amazing story. She nodded at her husband. "Orval had an uncle named Alfred. Orval's father, Harry, and Alfred were brothers. They both grew up on the family farm, and like many folks back then, they married two sisters. Alfred loved farming and particularly loved his horses. He had matched teams of Percherons, eight in all, and always prided himself on keeping the horses and their harness looking fine." Orval added that Alfred just wouldn't use a tractor; instead he'd take two teams out in the field every morning. Moving horses from task to task, he'd use four horses to pull the grain binder, three to pull the plow, and two to pull the cultivator or hay mower.

Some forty years ago, Alfred had driven his truck to town

to run an errand. At dusk, he pulled out of a driveway right in front of another vehicle and was struck on the driver's side. He was taken to the closest hospital, North Memorial, and was listed in critical condition.

JoAnn added, "In those days family members could visit for only five minutes at a time. I went in to visit the next afternoon and knew he wasn't doing well. A number of family members had gathered there, to keep watch and to pray.

"Orval had gone home to milk the cows, and I stayed to take Uncle Alfred's wife home. After dropping her off on the other side of Elk River, I was driving home down County Road 24, just past our neighbor's farm. I remember feeling sad and tired by the day's events. As I pulled to the intersection near home, I looked to the right across the hay field and saw our barn. That field had always been Uncle Alfred's favorite. He loved the way the land gently rolled.

"That's when I noticed a man walking across the hay field. He seemed bathed in soft, bright light that followed his footsteps." She paused and looked visibly distressed.

"You didn't know, but Uncle Alfred had a crippled hand; he had caught it in machinery a long time ago. He always carried that hand a little differently, and the man walking across the field held his hand the same way. And he wore a hat, you know, one with a bill, just exactly like the one Alfred used to wear. I couldn't believe my eyes!

"I slowed my car down since he looked different but somehow familiar. He slowed slightly and, without looking at me, he walked down into the roadside ditch, then up and *through* my car onto the field on the other side of the road. I noticed the light that surrounded him, unlike anything I had seen before. The light followed him as he walked north over near our neighbor Vic Roden's barn. I was surprised — actually, I was stunned. I didn't know what to think. It looked like Uncle Alfred but he seemed to be walking north, away from the farm.

"I can't even remember the short drive home. I ran up to the house; Orval met me at the door, took one look at me, and said, 'What's wrong?' "

JoAnn had stammered, "I just saw Uncle Alfred. He was walking in his favorite field followed by a light; then he walked north across the road, right through the front of my car!"

Orval looked stunned and said, "JoAnn, I got a phone call from the hospital — Alfred just died."

"You know, he was in a big bright, soft light. You can still see it. Come quick!"

Orval looked out, and he, too, saw a bright light near the field. Quickly he got on the phone and called his father, Harry, who lived across the street. "Dad, look out the window. What do you see out past Alfred's favorite field?"

Harry put down the phone, then returned a few minutes later. "I see a light out there to the north, just past Al's field, Orval."

"Thanks, Dad," Orval replied and hung up to comfort his wife.

After a few minutes, Orval called his father back. "Dad, look again, do you still see it? Do you think it's the moon?"

Harry looked out the window and then said, "No, son, it's way too big to be the moon, and it's still there. Besides that, the moon is coming up to the east!" When Harry checked a few minutes later, he reported the light was gone.

"What an amazing experience, JoAnn!" I said.

JoAnn looked thoughtful. "You know, it was so unusual, I really didn't know what to make of it."

Orval said, "We even called the police, and they told us that there was no problem in that field. Then a minister stopped to visit us a couple days after Alfred's death. We told him what happened in Alfred's favorite field. I asked what he thought, and without hesitation he said, 'I think God let you know that Alfred is on his way to heaven.'"

Some time went by as we sat at the kitchen table. JoAnn blotted the tears from her eyes. "I thought I was going crazy. I thought I had lost my mind."

"What do you think now?" I persisted.

"Well," she paused, "there is not a day that goes by that when I go past that field I don't think of Uncle Alfred. As time has passed, I've realized it wasn't my imagination; it really was him. I remember," she said, "the crops had all been taken in that previous fall; he died in the spring when the field was clean and ready for summer sun. Spring was always his favorite time of year.

"Some days I'm not sure," she said, pausing, "but now I think I'm beginning to see the whole picture."

WE PASSED
IN THE STORM

Later that evening as we sat around the kitchen table, Orval related another experience to me, a story passed down by his great-uncle Herman, his father's uncle. The story takes place over a hundred years ago in rural Worthington, Minnesota, where Herman Leistico and his family farmed the land.

In 1888, there was a severe blizzard, with high winds and heavy snow. In those days, thirty-foot-high drifts were not uncommon. Fiercely cold temperatures followed the blizzard, making travel almost impossible.

Two bachelor brothers, Harry and Walter Swenson, worked a dairy farm in the area and were friends with Orval's great-uncle Herman. As Orval explained, back then in the farming communities, they all depended on one another to help with threshing in the fall and planting in the spring. As a result, neighbors usually knew each other quite well. One late February day, Walter had driven to town with a team of horses and unfortunately got caught in the snowstorm while coming home with supplies. With high gusty winds, the storm quickly turned into a severe blizzard. Snow fell rapidly, and the wind blew the flakes so hard they became like needles. Walter and his team became disoriented; soon they were lost. When he did not return home that evening as expected, his brother, Harry, became worried. He began looking for him as best he could on foot, and several neighbors joined in the search.

The storm lasted over three days, during which time nobody saw any sign of Walter or the team. Harry was quite distressed but felt sure he would find him in time. He hoped that Walter had put up at a neighboring farm. When the storm finally subsided, it was followed by deadly cold temperatures with bitterly clear skies. Harry was out in the barn milking cows the following day, when, as he reported to anyone who would listen, he looked up and saw his brother, Walter, walk in. Harry was overjoyed and surprised and said, "Walter, what took you so long? It's about time you showed up!" Walter looked at him and said, "Harry, I thought you had been looking long enough. Me and the team, we passed in the storm." Harry blinked, and his brother was gone.

When Orval had finished, I paused for a moment, then said, "What do you make of it?"

"Oh," he said, "it scared me when I was a kid. But now it just makes me wonder." He looked down. "There are some things we just don't know.

"I always remember my dad's uncle telling me that Walter

Swenson and his wagon and team of horses were found down in a creek bed about a week later; they were frozen solid. You know, I've begun to think everyone has a story like this. It's just that until recently, everyone was afraid to talk about it. I think it's time we did; it changes you. You realize we don't have it all figured out. You remember to do the best you can with the day you've got. That's what will change the world, Janis."

PART V

THE FOURTH SECRET
WE ARE ALL CONNECTED

The universe is one indivisible and dynamic whole
in which energy and matter are so deeply entangled
it is impossible to consider them as independent elements.

— BRUCE LIPTON, PhD, *THE BIOLOGY OF BELIEF*

AN INTRICATE WEB
OF CONNECTIONS

It may be that once we begin to remember these familiar patterns, we see things differently and we awaken. Our remembering alerts our awareness. It is truly like looking at an optical illusion: one moment we see the trees, and the next moment the horses. And we wonder what changed. Of course, it is our awareness. Recognition triggers awareness; awareness causes perception, the foundation of intuition. Our perceptions influence thoughts, words, and actions — in other words, our conscious behavior.

Awareness can come to you as softly as a butterfly or as the warming of your face in the morning sun. But sometimes it jostles you awake like a gust of wind ahead of a fast-moving storm.

As a scientist and forensic pathologist, I could not *prove* the validity of these experiences to a reasonable degree of medical certainty, at least not with the tools I have been taught to use.

In fact, many times I have laughed at myself because, it seemed, they could not be proved at all.

However, hidden within these experiences is a magical, very familiar quality that fires up an ancient part of our being, one almost forgotten over time. The telling of an extraordinary experience, dream, or vivid vision jolts us back to remembering what it seems we once knew to be true and must have used daily.

What is this quality, one that shifts us from the thought that "seeing is believing" to "believing is seeing"? The answer is coming from a surprising source: quantum physicists and cell biologists.

Scientists are beginning to delve into the mysteries of cellular energy and explain what many intuitively know, that we are beings made up of body, mind, and spirit, and all are connected. The ability to understand and perceive energetic signals seems to be at the heart of the matter. When Einstein wrote, "The most beautiful thing we can experience is the mysterious," perhaps he already sensed the incredible beauty and wonder that comes from unfolding the secrets of energy and life. Scientists have begun to apply Einstein's wisdom to biological systems. Let me attempt to explain.

Einstein recognized that energy and matter are related; in fact, they are really the same thing. He put his thoughts together in his famous equation, $E = mc^2$. E stands for energy, m for mass, and c for the speed of light. Energy equals mass times the speed of light squared. In other words, mass can change form and become energy — an amount of energy that is equal to itself multiplied by the speed of light squared (the speed of light times the speed of light). This can represent an enormous amount of energy!

Scientists have begun to see that physical atoms are made up of whirling bits of energy, which are constantly oscillating and vibrating. This gives each atom its own unique energy pattern. Since molecules are composed of atoms, and organisms are composed of molecules, it follows that every material structure and every *body radiates* its own unique energy pattern.

Why is it that sometimes we "sense" or perceive things we do not see? The answers are being uncovered by science. I am fascinated by the work of cell biologists, and I highly recommend an elegant and approachable book by Bruce Lipton, PhD, *The Biology of Belief.* Lipton has shown that protein receptors on the membranes of individual cells actually respond to signals in their environment, both physical *and* energetic (light, sound, radio frequencies, the presence of another cell at a distance). The cellular signals are often located away from the cell yet close enough to be sensed.

These environmental signals actually activate and change cellular behavior. In other words, the receptors on the cell membranes make each cell *aware of* the elements in its environment. These protein receptors perceive the environment; in Lipton's phrase, they are the "fundamental units of cellular intelligence."[*]

Environmental signals, both physical and energetic, cause real effects; cells *react*, or *take action*. If cells can perceive and react to energy signals, it follows that other organisms, including humans, can as well. In fact, we do it all the time; we just don't recognize it. Who hasn't walked into a room and suddenly

---

[*] Bruce Lipton, *The Biology of Belief: Unleashing the Power of Consciousness, Matter and Miracles* (Santa Rosa, CA: Mountain of Love/Elite Books, 2005), p. 87.

felt welcome and comfortable? Or become aware of danger moments before it was apparent? Our bodies have an incredible built-in sensing ability. Some call it intuition. I believe it is the ability of our bodies to recognize energetic fields.

One thing more. We all know that the more we use any part of our body, the better, the stronger it gets, whether it is memory, muscles, or our level of awareness. Recognizing our ability and using it allows us to refine it. We begin to function more efficiently and differently. Our perceptions can influence our thoughts and feelings, even our bodies and health.

Why do "extraordinary experiences" seem so familiar and call to mind experiences that were previously unrecognized?

Dr. Bruce Lipton postulates that humans may have become so dependent on scientific proof that our ancient ability to perceive energy has been forgotten. Perhaps the recounting of extraordinary experiences rekindles our memory, triggering our ability to remember and recognize their energetic signature.

However it happens, you *know* it. Your perceptions are different, richer, and fuller; once you become aware, life is never the same again.

There is something magical about this quality, as with a garden. The more you tend it, the more it grows and becomes beautiful. With each passing year it matures. And in the end, the garden becomes wildly free, expressing itself fully and with wonder.

Perhaps it is no coincidence that nature is such a deep and authentic metaphor for life, and through it we begin to see the connections everywhere.

Of course, that, too, changes everything.

THE SEER

Afer a lecture on a beautiful early summer day at the Crest-
view Senior Living Center, many people crowded up to
talk. Among them were several executives and even a local minister. I listened intently as they commented and shared stories
of their own.

As the group dispersed, I looked longingly at the remain-
ing blueberry pastries sitting by the coffee. I had left early that
morning, and although I had indulged in a latte at the local
drive-through, I had not eaten breakfast. As I moved toward
the table, I noticed a woman near the edge of the room. She
looked at me hesitatingly and smiled shyly. She had a beautiful
face and chocolate-colored skin.

I smiled back encouragingly, and she said, "My name is
Theresa. I have had many of those experiences."

I sensed a richness and quiet grace about this woman. "The hospice program where I volunteer told me about your lecture," she said.

We paused a moment. I heard the noisy sound of metal chairs being folded. Out of the corner of my eye I saw the chairs being stacked on a cart by the men of the cleanup crew.

She hesitated. "I am glad you came today," I offered. I realized that my path to the pastry table had been interrupted, but there was something about this woman that made me stop. I felt she had something to say.

"There is a gift in my family that is passed down, the gift of seeing. I have it too."

As I moved a step closer to her, the noise all around us faded away.

"I would like to tell you about one of the most extraordinary experiences I have had."

"I would be honored," I said.

"I used to work at the Early Learning Center here in Minneapolis as a preschool teacher," she began. "Three of us women who worked there became very good friends. Marge was one of the other teachers, and Joyce drove the school bus. We often hung out together. It felt like we were sisters!

"One night I had the most beautiful dream. I saw Marge as plain as day, and she said to me, 'Theresa, come with me shopping. I have to pick out some things.' The next thing I knew, we were off somewhere in a dressing room, and Marge had put on a beautiful maroon dress. She twirled around. The color complimented her eyes, and her skin just glowed. 'How do you think it looks?' she asked. 'Just beautiful,' I replied.

"'One more thing,' Marge said, and she fastened a delicate lacy round locket on a gold chain around her neck. 'You look wonderful,' I told her, and we danced around each other with joy. She just burst with happiness. I remember I woke briefly after my extraordinary dream and saw it was midnight.

"When I awakened that next morning, I was overcome with such a sense of peace. I felt refreshed and calm. The feeling left a mark on my memory, and I have not forgotten.

"That day started off like all the rest — that is, until Joyce knocked on my apartment door. She looked alarmed and upset. 'Did you hear about Marge?' she asked urgently. 'No, I didn't!' I exclaimed, taking a step back.

"'She had a heart attack last night and died!'

"'Oh, *no!*' I said as tears began to run down my face. I was devastated and cried at the loss of my best friend. Joyce leaned forward to comfort me with a hug. 'When — I mean, what time did it happen?'

"'About midnight,' Joyce answered.

"'What? Oh, no.' I was shocked, stunned. I couldn't believe that Marge, my good friend, was dead.

"The rest of the day was a blur. I don't remember anything much until I went to the mortuary with Joyce the following afternoon. But what happened next I will never forget.

"When I turned the corner and entered the room where her body lay, I was riveted by what I saw. Marge's body lay beautifully still, clad in a flowing maroon dress with a round lacy gold locket around her neck. I burst into tears, now remembering my beautiful dream.

"I couldn't stay there any longer, the connection and the

remembrance were so strong and still so painfully fresh. It was only later I discovered what was in the locket. It was a photo of Marge's daughter."

Theresa wiped a tear from the corner of her eye as she finished her story.

"Thank you, Theresa!" I said. "What an extraordinary experience, and what a gift!"

"You are welcome, Doctor. I knew you would understand."

"Theresa, I have a question." She nodded. "I know you were shocked at first, but how did you feel later?"

"That one is easy," she said with a laugh. "I felt blessed, so incredibly blessed. Full and rich, and affirmed in everything I already know."

Then she added apologetically, "I can't afford your book right now, but I will soon."

"Here," I said, "this one is for you," as I wrote her name inside the cover. "Thank you for sharing that with me," I said from the bottom of my heart.

As for the blueberry pastries, by the time I looked again, they were gone, but it didn't matter. I had gotten a much better treat.

DO YOU REMEMBER D-DAY?

Gray hair formed curls around the intensely clear brown eyes of the woman who introduced herself as Liz and asked, "Do you remember D-day?"

"Of course," I said with the slightest uncertainty, searching my memory. "June 6th, wasn't it?"

"My brother Robert died there in France on D-day," Liz said as she handed me a book about the heroic actions of the Allies and specifically the U.S. forces in that invasion in 1944. I opened the book to see the face of Robert Style, a young and handsome man whose brown eyes echoed his sister's. "I had three brothers. William served in the Pacific on a ship near New Guinea and in the Philippines; he survived the war and was sent home. My other brother, Jim, died in the Battle of the Bulge when a bazooka hit his tank four days after Christmas 1944.

"Bob was in the 101st Airborne, the 501st Division, the men who parachuted behind enemy lines the night before the surprise attack. He was a tall, gangly kid, very athletic, about 6 feet tall and only 175 pounds. The paratroopers were highly trained — they had to be — in hand-to-hand combat and survival. You probably don't remember the details of the invasion of Normandy…"

"No, I don't; tell me," I said.

"Well," she began, "the Germans had driven out the Allies and seized control of France. Then the Allies, which included France, Great Britain, the United States, and Canada, planned an invasion of France to liberate Europe from the German forces. They decided to begin the invasion by landing the army on the northwest coast of France, on the beaches of Normandy. My brother was one of the many paratroopers who were dropped behind German lines the night before the landing. Their job was to surprise and attack the Germans from behind, helping those who would land on the beach.

"On the night of June 6th, my mother had a dream, a dream that she didn't tell us about until much later. She did, however, remember it vividly. She saw my brother's hands — they were cupped — and she heard him say to her, 'Don't worry, Mom; I am okay.'

"Along with the rest of the country, we found out about the events of D-day on the radio as they unfolded. It wasn't until two weeks later that we received a telegram stating that Bob was missing in action. I remember how we worried and thought about him during the days that followed. Then several weeks later two uniformed men knocked on our front door and told my mom and me that Robert had been killed on June 6th, D-day, in France. The details were sketchy. Another telegram was sent to Mom and Dad at the end of July 1944, informing them of Bob's death and telling them that he had been buried at Sainte Mère Église. It was only then Mom shared her dream with us."

Liz's voice was calm and strong. "Mother had Bob's body moved from Sainte Mère Église to Henri Chapelle American Cemetery near Liege, Belgium, to be placed beside his older brother, Jim. We visited their graves in 1949.

"Some time later, after both my mom and dad had died, my surviving brother, William, found out what really happened from one of the men in Bob's unit. Bob and two others had landed after parachuting in at night. Bob was acting as the scout and was ahead of the others. He was crawling through a muddy ditch into a hedgerow when one of the grenades attached to his flak vest got caught on a twig, and the pin dislodged from the grenade.

"One of the men remembered Bob's eyes being fixed on the grenade. My brother attempted to replace the pin, but when he realized it wouldn't work, he cupped the grenade in his hands, curled his body around it, and took the blast so that his friends and fellow soldiers would live. When I remembered mother's dream and Bob's hands, I knew he was letting us know...know that he was fine.

"Several years ago, William was contacted by a Dutch farmer in the Netherlands who served in France during World

War II. Shortly after D-day, this Dutchman found a helmet, a glasses case, and other personal effects in a ditch near a hedge-row. He traced them to Bob Styles and generously returned them to our family."

Now, thanks to Liz's story, I, too, will never forget D-day and the events that unfolded. And as always, I will wonder what really happened.

BRIANNA'S BUTTERFLIES

Nothing means anything except the meaning we give it.

— NEALE DONALD WALSCH

The Mercy Hospital Cardiac Rehabilitation Center is a very rich collection of people and stories — rich, in part, because of the wonderful camaraderie and kinship of the staff; rich, also, because of their wisdom and sense of humor. These folks rarely miss a day of exercise; they are profoundly aware of the consequences of ignoring the health of their bodies and minds and have a keen appreciation for another day of life. My dear friend Bill Hoogestrat used to say, "Janis, learn from your experiences so you will grow wise. You see, you can either live one year seventy times, or you can live seventy years!"

One evening, on my way out after exercising at the end of the day, I recognized one of the regulars there, a hospital volunteer named Gary, who waved at me with a smile. "Hey, Doc, I have a story for you." He pulled a wrinkled piece of paper out of his pocket. "Here, I wrote this out for you." I took the paper from his hand. "Thanks," I said.

"This means a lot to me, Doc. I know these experiences are true. And the more I am aware of them, the more I see."

I nodded in agreement. "When you know it, you see it."

I got back to my office, pulled his note out of my pocket, and began to read:

My friend's daughter was killed August 13, 1986, on her birthday; she was just thirteen years old. Brianna was walking her bicycle across the road and was struck by a car. She died a few hours later at the hospital. Her whole family was just devastated. None of us could believe it had really happened. Her funeral service was packed with friends and family members. But it was at the grave site service at Forest Hill Cemetery that day I experienced something I will never forget.

It was a brilliantly sunny, cloudless blue-sky day filled with the rich green shades of high summer. We had come in a long procession from the church to the cemetery. The parked cars seemed to stretch endlessly down the narrow graveyard road. Many people gathered around while the pastor spoke and then concluded the prayer service. Family members and friends draped Brianna's casket with flowers, and then we stood there wordlessly.

The pungent smell of the pine trees overhead mingled with the fragrance of the flowers in the faint summer breeze. Most of us were reluctant to leave and lingered there awhile in the dappled shade and sunlight. The mourners began to slowly filter back to their cars until only a few of us were left. After what seemed a long time, Brianna's parents, my dear friends, turned to leave, and I followed behind. We had walked no more than twenty feet when, for no reason except perhaps my intuition, I stopped and glanced back one more time.

To my surprise and astonishment, above her casket forty or fifty Monarch butterflies hovered protectively. Some had lit on the flowers; others had gently landed on the velvet-draped casket. A number of butterflies hung almost motionless above her grave. I glanced back and saw Brianna's parents had also stopped and turned around. Their eyes, too, were riveted on the spot, and their faces were etched with amazement. I glanced at the other graves and stone markers to my right and left but couldn't see another butterfly. The sudden appearance of these majestic Monarchs seemed almost surreal, and I noticed that others, too, had stopped to look. It was especially poignant because Brianna loved butterflies.

Nobody spoke for quite some time; it was a very moving and comforting experience. Her family even had a butterfly engraved on her tombstone in memory of the event.

One year later her father, my friend Ted, asked me to go with him to visit her grave. It was the anniversary of her birthday and death, August 13. The day was hot, sunny, and still. We parked near her grave, walked up, and stood there for a few moments. The year had been a difficult one for Ted and his family. A few moments passed, and I heard a faint stirring. From behind us, a large cloud of Monarch butterflies suddenly appeared; they hovered over Brianna's grave, and many of them lighted on her gravestone. Ted and I both had goose bumps as we stood there silently and took it all in. We noticed that both times the Monarchs hovered over her grave and no place else.

The next time I saw Gary, I stopped to talk. "Do you think it was a coincidence, Doctor?" he asked.

"No," I replied, "I don't think so."

We were both silent for a brief period of time. "What do you think, Gary?" I asked. "And what did your friend Ted, Brianna's dad, think?"

"Well, Doc, I think it saved his life."

I nodded slowly and understood.

PART VI

THE FIFTH SECRET
THERE IS NO NEED TO FEAR

Life is perfectly safe.

— MARSHALL BUSH

NO FEAR

In the end, what matters most is not the years in your life, but the life in your years.

— ABRAHAM LINCOLN

My foray into the Cardiac Rehab Center to exercise on a bright, clear Friday afternoon in September last year led me to the treadmills, where several of the instructors were working out. The rhythmic pace of their feet helped pull me through twenty-five sweaty minutes.

As I was finishing, an older man with slightly graying hair, in exercise clothes and with a towel around his neck, walked up to me tentatively with the words, "Excuse me but are you the coroner?"

"Why, yes, I am, although I don't usually look like this..." I said with a rather breathless smile, acutely aware of the sweat dripping off my face and nose.

"You wrote the book, didn't you?"

"Yes," I nodded, "I did."

"I read it, and so did my wife," he said. "You know, Doctor, what you wrote about is true for me." I immediately noticed his choice of words, "true for me." They seemed to be coming from his heart.

"Thank you."

"You know, my wife had an experience," he said, looking down quickly. "Her first husband died suddenly and unexpectedly of a heart condition. Shortly thereafter, her mother-in-law became gravely ill and was hospitalized, and my wife visited her every day. She told me later that one night she was awakened by a phone call in the middle of the night. When she picked up the phone, the voice was unmistakable — it was her first husband, who had died so recently, and he said to her, 'Mary, don't worry. Mother is with me now.' When she woke the following morning, she remembered the phone call, but she dismissed it — until later, when she called the hospital and found that her mother-in-law had died sometime in the middle of the night. She had been found by nursing staff in the morning."

"What is your name?" I asked.

"Marshall Bush," he said. His brown eyes had begun to well up with tears.

"Thank you for sharing that with me," I said. "What a beautiful story."

"My wife really knows she heard the phone ring. It wasn't a dream."

"I know," I said. "It doesn't matter."

"Doctor," he said, "all these stories, your book, my wife's experience — I *know* they are true."

"How do they make you feel?" I asked, "I mean, have they changed your life in any way?"

"I have no fear; now I live without fear. You know," he said, "recently a friend of mine was dying from cancer. He comforted me when he said, 'Don't worry, Marshall. I'm just going on to the next chapter.'"

"In the book of life," I added.

Marshall smiled and said, "Yes."

I walked over to begin lifting a few weights, smiling to myself at the treasure I had just received.

And I thought — perhaps there are many chapters in the book of life, more than we know. That's why it's called the "book of life," and we are immortals.

THE LAST LAUGH

Laugh, and the world laughs with you...

D r. Paul Sanders is a family practice physician and friend who practiced medicine for over forty years at a rural hospital where I worked for a time as the laboratory director. I always loved talking with him, for his keen mind never stopped asking questions, and his keen wit never missed a beat.

He is retired now but still active in the Minnesota Medical Association (MMA) in our central chapter, where he also served as president. Recently I saw him at the fall MMA meeting, where I lectured on the subject of these extraordinary experiences to a group of physicians. Although it was the last lecture of the weekend seminar and a beautiful crisp autumn day, the group listened attentively. I was very pleased, since occasionally lecturing to my sometimes skeptical peers can be difficult.

Dr. Sanders waited for me outside the conference room that day, and with a cryptic smile on his face, he said, "I have a story to tell you. In 1974 my father, Sidney, was diagnosed with prostate cancer that had already spread to the bone. My dad was a wonderful man who always loved a good laugh. When our family would gather, he would often tell so many funny stories and jokes that we would double over with laughter, our sides aching and tears running down our faces. We would sometimes laugh for hours, and Dad was always in the middle of it.

"I had felt that something was wrong that year, since I noticed he didn't tell his funny stories, and I couldn't remember the last time I heard him laugh. When the diagnosis was made, I began to understand. Tumor in bone is extremely painful. You know, it's only been recently we have learned how to keep those patients comfortable.

"His last days were hard. That was before hospice care, and he lived alone since Mom had died a few years earlier. The pain and the loneliness robbed him of his usual laughter and joy in living.

"When he was admitted to the Cambridge Hospital for pain control, I knew he was near the end. I remember I had just arrived home from work one evening when the phone rang, and the nurse told me that Dad had suffered a cardiac arrest. Those were the days too before the patient directives and do not resuscitate orders were in place. My good friend and colleague, Dr. Carston Seacamp, had begun CPR, and I rushed to the hospital, my heart pounding.

"I leaped out of my car and ran frantically down the hall to his room. As I got to the doorway something quite extraordinary happened.

"I glanced to my left and saw my father's motionless body lying in bed, ringed by nurses with their backs to me. Carston was on the other side of the bed, intently doing CPR. He glanced up quickly as I stopped in the doorway. I was still breathing heavily from my run up the hospital steps and along the hallway. And just at that moment, I was startled when to my right I *heard* more than sensed the absolutely unmistakable sound of my father's booming laugh. It was bold, gleeful, and joyful, that wonderful sound I hadn't heard in so many months as he suffered with his disease. My heart jumped with joy.

"I knew in that instant that he was fine, and I turned to my friend Carston and said confidently, 'Let him go.'

"Carston was looking at me keenly. 'Oh, so you heard him, too!' he said as the nurses looked at us with puzzled eyes. I knew something extraordinary had happened and that we had witnessed a miracle. I miss my father greatly, but I will never forget the sound of his laughter and the experience of awesome joy as I walked into that room. Perhaps, Dr. Amatuzio, we really don't remember what is waiting for us, but I have a feeling there is nothing to fear."

DR. LYON
AND MY FATHER

I received a letter from Dr. Frederick Lyon, a retired obstetrician-gynecologist. Since he mentioned that he had known my father well, I shared it with my dad the following weekend when I visited. Dr. Lyon's experience and the one my father then told shared similarities — beginning with a sense of certainty, calm, and knowing. Both men are respected retired physicians; both have the air of elder statesmen. Their words were delivered with the familiar ring of a confidant diagnosis.

Dr. Lyon had written:

Many years ago, I suffered an acute myocardial infarct which was followed by severe angina, or chest pain. My own physician recommended coronary angiography, which resulted in my having triple aorto-coronary bypass surgery.

After many months of recovery at home, I was finally able to start back into practice.

One Sunday morning I was called to the old Mount Sinai Hospital in Minneapolis. A colleague requested a consultation and I gladly responded. We quickly resolved the medical issue.

I returned to my automobile in the doctors' lot, turned the key, and shifted into reverse. I turned my head, looking over my right shoulder to make certain all was clear for backing out, when all of a sudden I found myself looking down a long, dark tunnel. A most intense and vibrant light was visible at the far end of the tunnel. I was surrounded by the most incredible heavenly, celestially beautiful music. Every color of the rainbow, the most magnificent hues, danced around me.

I experienced absolute, total peace and serenity. I felt no fear, no apprehension or danger. I was overwhelmed with a sense of calm, wonder, and awe. I was absolutely astonished.

When I "awoke," I found that I had driven down a long driveway, made a right turn, crossed a busy street, and wedged my front bumper against a tree in the park across from the hospital. The car wasn't damaged in spite of the fact that I must have been stopped by the impact. I have no recollection or explanation of how I managed to drive my car such a distance without being aware of the act of driving.

After taking a few minutes to assess what had happened, I drove home. I was bewildered and somewhat anxious; I could not comprehend the sequence of events.

My wife had invited several friends over for Sunday brunch, but I needed to lie down in a quiet room for several minutes to collect my thoughts — and myself. I joined the company for brunch later without disclosing my experience. Only later did I tell my wife.

I have no explanation for the experience. I have always wondered if I experienced an abnormal heart rhythm resulting in momentary cardiac arrest or arrhythmia. Or if I awkwardly twisted my neck and constricted a carotid blood vessel causing sudden brain anoxia, or lack of oxygen.

I fully understand what you meant when you wrote about the sheriff who, after nearly drowning, told you, "Dying is easy. It's living that counts." Since that experience, I have no fear of dying. I have used my experience to comfort several friends and patients who were terminally ill.

I READ DR. LYON'S LETTER to my father as we sat at the kitchen table while my mother made lunch.

"I remember Dr. Lyon well," he said with a smile. "We had such a good medical staff at Mt. Sinai Hospital, and Fred was a very good doctor! His experience sounds a little like mine, Janis."

"What experience, Dad?" I said with surprise.

He paused for a moment. "Do you remember when I was a patient there?" he asked, looking at my mother.

"Do I remember!" she exclaimed. "It was 1955 or 1956; Janis was four, and Barry was just a few months old."

Dad continued, "I had been having very severe abdominal pain for three to four days. I couldn't even get out of bed."

"And he wouldn't get any help," my mother added. "So I called his friend, the surgeon Dr. Lyle Hay. He stopped after work that day to examine Don."

"I remember," my father said. "He said, 'Don, let's take a ride to the hospital. I would like to get a few tests and X-rays.' I agreed with him and got up to get dressed."

Mother said, "I told him, 'Let me come with you,' and Lyle said, 'Verda, stay home and care for your babies. I'll take good care of him.'"

"Good care!" my father chortled. "He hit every bump in the road and every railroad track on the way to Mt. Sinai, and it hurt like heck every time! But I knew what that meant and so did he — classic symptoms of inflammation of the abdominal wall when something has ruptured."

Something had indeed ruptured: a diverticulum, a pouching-out in the wall of the small intestine, had become inflamed and burst, causing intestinal contents to spill into the abdominal cavity. Dad was taken immediately to surgery. The abdominal cavity was filled with pus, and the intestines were severely inflamed. Dr. Hay removed the ruptured diverticulum and completed the surgery. But Dad was sicker than anyone had suspected.

His inflamed intestines had stopped functioning, were essentially paralyzed, and no nutrients were being absorbed by his body. This was a condition not compatible with survival.

"How did you feel, Dad?" I asked. "I mean, do you remember?"

He looked thoughtful. "Oh yes, I remember. I knew that I

was seriously ill, but I only really got concerned after surgery when I had no appetite and couldn't keep any fluids or even Jell-O down. I remember my dear friend Dr. Hay coming to see me each day and reassuring me that it would just take time for the inflammation to subside and my intestines to begin working again.

"Each morning he would sit by my bedside with the door closed, place his stethoscope on my abdomen, and listen for bowel sounds, some sign that my intestines had started to function again. Sometimes he would come back in the evening and listen for another half hour. I knew he was concerned as the days passed into a week, then into the second week. And so was I . . . I knew that if my intestines didn't start soon, I would die."

"But you told me that something happened to you there, something mysterious," I said.

"Well, something did happen to me one afternoon. I told your mother about it at the time."

Mother smiled and nodded. "You did, and I remember how amazed you were after that and how calm."

"Tell me, Dad," I persisted.

"You know, Janis, I have always kept it a secret . . ."

I sat there in the kitchen and waited. Dad rocked a little in his glider chair.

"I didn't see any white light or tunnel. I had fallen asleep in the middle of the afternoon, The nurses had drawn the window shades — and then I left!"

"What do you mean, Dad?"

"Janis, I just left. It was just that simple. I was fully aware and clear in my mind. I had the sense of leaving that hospital room and traveling across a vast space in what seemed like — seconds! I was moving effortlessly, flying." He smiled.

"I arrived at the most magnificent place I could ever remember. It was green and lush, the colors were so vivid, and there was the most beautiful music I have ever heard. It filled the place. The light there just glowed, so bright and so gentle. It was so familiar.

"Then I came to a river. I could see to the other side. There were all my family and friends who had died on the other shore, my father and grandfather, and someone else, a male figure that was so familiar. They were so happy to see me. They all waved and beckoned me across. I was overjoyed and began to wade the river.

"Then I noticed that one by one they stopped waving and turned around, putting their backs to me. I stopped and realized in an instant that I was not to cross over."

He stopped rocking and looked down. "I don't know how much time had passed, but when I awakened, it was early evening. I remember feeling so astonished and amazed at what had just happened. A sense of profound peacefulness and calm seemed to fill my hospital room and me."

Mother looked at him. "You told me about your experience when I came to visit the next day. You said you were so happy to see your father again. Do you remember the rest of it, Don?"

"Yes, Verda, how could I forget? Lyle, my faithful friend and surgeon, came to see me that evening. He closed the door, once again placed his stethoscope on my abdomen, and began to listen. I watched his brow begin to furrow as he repositioned the stethoscope several times.

"Then a big smile spread across his face. 'Don!' he said. 'Your intestines are working! You're going to be okay!' And for the first time in my life I saw my physician and friend put his hand to his face and cry."

THE BLUE HEALER

Kizzie was a "healer" in every sense of the word, but mostly because a healer makes you whole.

She started life as a black-haired, silver-sprinkled puppy, a gift to Denise from her father when she left home for her first job. The black-and-silver color made Kizzie's coat seem blue; the innate ability to herd sheep and cattle by nipping at their heels gave rise to the name of her breed, blue heeler.

Denise is a professional equestrian who rides and shows horses all over the United States. Intuitive, bright, and tough, she dedicates her life to the highest quality of equine care and to the education of horse owners. Her greatest skill is her uncanny ability to "see" from the horse's point of view and to diagnose disease and injury. Those lucky horses in her care glow and sparkle with health from head to tail, and they perform willingly and well.

For ten years Kizzie was Denise's constant companion, going everywhere Denise went, and she seemed to understand every mood and word. It wasn't uncommon at the end of the day to find Denise sitting on a bench with Kizzie beside her, muzzle pressed into Denise's leg, looking soulfully into Denise's eyes. Whenever anyone sat down next to Denise, Kizzie would slowly but steadily work her way between them until she had wedged herself right up against Denise's side.

In 1991, Denise decided to move back to her home state of Minnesota and establish her business here. Kizzie was twelve years old then, still fit and happy. But as she grew older, she developed progressive kidney failure, managed at first by diet, then by medications, but eventually it began taking its toll. Denise felt anguished, but when the time came, she made the decision that there would be no more therapy; Kizzie would be taken home.

Kizzie spent her last days on blankets at the foot of Denise's bed. It was a Saturday evening when Kizzie slowly got up, walked over, and gazed up intently at Denise with her big brown eyes. Then she moved a few steps back, lay down, and calmly took her last breath.

Although Kizzie's death was peaceful, Denise was overwhelmed with grief, both at the loss of her dear companion and with concern that perhaps her blue heeler had lingered too long and suffered. She was almost inconsolable until one night six months later when she had an amazing experience.

Actually, Denise would call the extraordinary dream a "visit," since it was unlike anything that had ever happened to her before — or has since. In her dream that night, Denise saw her beloved blue heeler, Kizzie. She shared her story with me after I put my own horses in her care some years later.

"Kizzie was running like she did when she was a puppy, with wild playfulness, in the most beautiful place imaginable — breathtaking, wide-open, colorful outdoor spaces that defy description. There were brilliantly colored flowers of every shade that filled up almost every inch of the ground and stretched as far as the eye could see. The colors were more vivid than I'd ever imagined — purples, yellows, pinks and reds, blues and greens that just shimmered.

"Kizzie was running and bouncing across the flowers in the field, so joyful and content," Denise said. "Then she saw me. Her tail wagged furiously, and she stopped suddenly with her front legs and tummy down on the ground, and her back end up in the air like she always did when she wanted my attention. Her big brown eyes looked deeply into mine, and without a sound, she let me know she was happy and this was a very, very good place. Then she gave me another gift. She told me to stop worrying about her now, as all was very well, and she would be there for me whenever I needed her.

"When I woke up, I instantly and absolutely *knew* she was fine, and my heart was healed, my grieving was over. It felt as though my innermost thoughts were completely rearranged and were strangely calm and peaceful."

However, another gift awaited Denise. The most profound moment of her life occurred several years later when she happened to rent the movie *What Dreams May Come*. In an astonishing experience of déjà vu, she saw a scene in the movie depicting the very same open, vibrant meadow filled with wildly colorful flowers that she had seen in her dream of Kizzie! Denise was stunned. And then the peace and joy she had experienced reawakened in her heart, and her surprise faded to the calm, still place of deep knowing.

When we spoke together about her profound experience, I asked what had changed in her life since then. Like so many others with the courage to look clearly beyond conventional belief, she said, "This experience has been so profound for me. Now I am certain: I *know* there is much more waiting for all of us after our brief visit here on earth. I have no fear."

Kizzie was truly a "blue healer."

MARY JANE'S DAD

The night was snowy and dark as I arrived at the community college to lecture to nursing students, and I went to the wrong auditorium.

The time for the lecture was fast approaching; the halls were dark and deserted. I realized I was in the wrong place and turned around to retrace my steps. Just then two young women walked right up to me and said, "Are you Dr. Amatuzio?" I nodded hopefully. "We are waiting for you in the other building, across campus."

With a sense of relief, I quickly followed them across campus and arrived at the lecture hall with only a minute to spare. I shed my coat and boots, walked in, and began my lecture on dreams, visions, and extraordinary experiences, and what impact they might have on these students' own perceptions and future practice of nursing.

When I finished, two nursing instructors walked up to me, waiting until I had finished speaking with several of the students. One of the instructors, Linda, commented that her father had recently died, but she was doing all right. Mary Jane, however, had tears in her eyes and said she had something to tell me. With some difficulty she told me the following story.

"My father died three years ago. He was in a hospice program, suffering from congestive heart failure and complications of diabetes. We grew up on a farm in Iowa, and Dad had never left the area except to serve in Europe and the Mediterranean during World War II. Dad's own father died in 1947, just after my dad had returned home from the war. My father faithfully worked the family farm, following in his dad's footsteps, literally.

"When Dad was in the terminal stages of his illness, he chose not to have any further medical intervention. We were fine with his decision, and since I am a nurse, he and my family depended heavily on me at that time. Dad's condition began to deteriorate. He was lapsing in and out of consciousness, sleeping most of the time, and no longer eating.

"Finally, one evening, just twelve hours before he died, I sat quietly with him, just he and I. He hadn't spoken for several days. He gently opened his eyes wide and smiled as he said, 'Pops, how good to see you.' Then the smile faded from his face and he seemed to drift back off to sleep. I hadn't heard him say 'Pops' for many years, not since his own father, my grandpa, had died.

"I said to him, 'Is Grandpa here?'

"He roused slightly, smiled, and replied, 'Oh, yes, he's been here several times.' Then he nodded slightly as if to reassure me that all was well.

"My father seemed filled with certain peacefulness and an astonishing calm, which also affected us, his family. Dad died peacefully the following morning. His words have comforted me greatly."

Although we miss our loved ones terribly at the time of their passing and feel especially that our relationships with our parents are among the most intimate, the frequent appearances of their own parents remind me of all the intimate relationships that have gone before — and the incredible circle of life. That may also be part of their gift to us—to remind us the passageway is safe, all is well, and there is no reason for fear.

Of course, that changes everything.

PART VII

THE SIXTH SECRET
ALL IS WELL

The wind always blows in the direction
of the Promised Land.

— RACHEL NAOMI REMEN,
MY GRANDFATHER'S BLESSINGS

THE SIXTH SECRET

ALL IS WELL

ALL IS WELL

The truth is, I have had qualms about the above title, "All Is Well." In my practice, many times all does *not* seem well: the death of a child, the violent murder of a young woman, or the motor vehicle crash that takes the lives of a married couple.

However, the extraordinary experiences so often brought to my attention, especially while practicing forensic pathology, have put me on another path, the path to my own truth. These experiences cause me to wonder and to open my heart to my own inner wisdom and sensibility. They lift me to a new level of clarity and understanding of life, and God — which seem to be names for the same thing.

Gradually, I have begun to trust myself, my intuition, and the process of life. I remember now that when you look closely enough at something, you begin to see right through it. I have begun to realize that life "is the stuff that dreams are made of." That realization allows any person to create a life filled with his or her own highest dreams and ideas. I know if all of us did that, it would change the world.

The chapter heading "All Is Well" expresses the truth that exists in my own heart when I am calm and clear, when I remember to be still. And that brings me to another place, a deep sense of peace.

This is the place I return to in meditation, when I feel weary and worn by the push and pull of my practice and demands of my life or when I miss someone who has died. Then I remember the words in the last chapter of a book that I treasure, *Their Eyes Were Watching God* by Zora Neale Hurston.

> Of course he wasn't dead. He could never be dead until she herself had finished feeling and thinking. The kiss of his memory made pictures of love and light against the wall. Here was peace. She pulled in her horizon like a great fish-net. Pulled it from around the waist of the world and draped it over her shoulder. So much of life in its meshes. She called in her soul to come and see.[*]

And I *know* then that *all is well*.

---

[*] Zora Neale Hurston, *Their Eyes Were Watching God* (New York: Harper Perennial, 1990), pp. 183–84.

CHARLOTTE'S BLESSING

Charlotte Johnson is an elegant woman and the beloved wife of R. W. Johnson, the former Anoka County attorney, who is in turn one of the most respected and brilliant attorneys and thinkers I have ever known. Charlotte and I have met numerous times; she has always had a kind word or reassuring compliment for me, particularly during the time I have been the Anoka County coroner. Recently, in what she calls her "wisdom years," she wrote me a letter about her mother, Sarah.

On January 8, 1991, my mother had a massive stroke at age ninety-five; this left her unable to move or speak. Macular degeneration [a condition in which deterioration of the retina of the eye leads to blindness] had robbed her of her sight several years earlier. My father had died twenty-five years before, and my mother missed him terribly. I knew she would not live long.

Mom was moved from her home to Guardian Angel's Nursing Home, where she had a bright, sunny single room. She was given medication to ease her pain, and I visited her every day. We spent many hours together. Sometimes I would just sit next to her bed; other times I would read to her or recall familiar scenes and events from our family. Although Mom couldn't speak or respond, I knew she heard me and I felt she appreciated my visits.

On February 7th at 9:30 A.M., the nursing home called and told me Mom was not far from death. I tried calling my brother right away, but couldn't reach him. My husband and I left immediately, and when we arrived, I went directly to my mother's room, only to find out she had been moved. I ran down the hall and found her in a smaller room with no windows and only the one door through which I entered. I didn't realize that my husband had stayed behind; I was there alone with Mom. The room was furnished just with Mom's bed and a chair. I sat down, looked at my mother's face, and caught my breath.

I sat that way for perhaps five or ten minutes thinking about Mom and her life. I was not grief-stricken. Instead I felt calm, realizing Mom's suffering was about to end and soon she would at last be with my father, her beloved Ted, and with my brother, who was killed in World War II. Mom had grieved for both her husband and her son for many years.

I sat there quietly and alone, listening to the slowing but rhythmic sound of her breathing. Suddenly I was startled and surprised to see, or more accurately to feel, a powerful whirlwind that entered the room from my left side and proceeded up to the head of the bed over my mother's still body. It hovered there for five or ten seconds. I was stunned and amazed — and utterly unprepared for what happened next.

From above and opposite the chair on which I sat, I felt her presence and clearly heard her voice for the first time since her stroke, a month earlier. She said in a quiet and gently reassuring voice, "Charlotte, I'm all right now. You go on and live your life." And then she was gone. I looked at her body and knew she had died. But what I had experienced, what really happened, astonished me.

I have relived this experience every day since Mother passed, and I continue to be amazed. I often wonder about the beautiful implications of what I know is a Very Great Blessing!

THE TALE
OF THE DRAGONFLY

This story was relayed to me by a woman who had invited me to lecture at a local church gathering. She told me she had used the story to explain death to her young son after the death of his uncle. It had become one of his favorites.

All the water bugs in the pond lived happy lives, swimming to and fro beneath the surface, raising families, and playing all day long. Rays of light would pierce their pond and turn the waters from forest green to turquoise to blue and back again. Lily pads floated peacefully on the surface. All the bugs knew that sometimes a water bug would be drawn to all the sparkling light up high and would swim to the edge of a lily pad and, with luck, climb on. For some reason, those particular water bugs never came back.

"What really happens on the lily pad?" they thought. One day a very smart, strong water bug set off to find out. She swam up and up to the sparkling light above. A big, inviting green lily pad stretched lazily across the surface. She grabbed hold and pulled herself up with a mighty heave. The sunlight was warm and the sky vibrantly blue and the breeze, oh, so gentle. She stretched out contentedly, peering down over the edge where she could see her family swimming busily to and fro, blissfully unaware of her presence. "Should I go back?" she thought. "Well, perhaps I'll stay here awhile. It's so warm and bright. I really like it here on the lily pad."

She fell asleep in the warm sunlight, and when she awakened she knew that something had changed. She had wings, she could fly, and she flew effortlessly over her pond. She soared and played and danced to and fro in the sunlight along the surface catching the breezes that tossed her to and fro, yet still aware of all the little water bugs in the beautiful waters below. And when she looked down, she saw her reflection. She gasped with astonishment at the breadth and beauty of her wings. And she saw herself for who she really was, a beautiful dragonfly with wings of many colors dancing on the wind and the wild.

With practice she discovered that she could gently touch the water's surface, alighting there for minutes as she lovingly looked at her water bug family below. She could see them, but they did not notice her. Many times she whispered to the sun and the wind and sent them her love. Some days she would fly close by to alight gently on the interface, the surface, the veil between her and them.

She wondered why they did not notice her, but then again, none of them looked up.

When I had finished reading this story, the woman told me her son was killed by a drunk driver when he was just nineteen years old. At his funeral a beautiful dragonfly lit on the lapel of her suit and remained there for many minutes. She knew.

"WHEN YOU NEED
A FRIEND..."

In 1996, Dr. Calvin Bandt retired from his position as the director of the clinical laboratories at Hennepin County Medical Center. Eighteen years had elapsed since he had peered into my microscope at the medical examiner's office and diagnosed ethylene glycol poisoning in an elderly depressed man. I attended his retirement party and wished him well. He was planning several trips with his family — as well as two trips to Bosnia. He had been invited to join an international group of scientists working to identify the remains of hundreds of bodies that had been discovered in mass graves in Bosnia and Serbia at the end of the war there. For Cal Bandt, retirement was not a time to slow down; it was simply a time to shift gears.

By 1996, I was the only forensic pathologist in the pathology group that covered both Mercy and Unity Hospitals. I was in charge of death investigation services for two large counties, Anoka and Wright. As 1997 drew to a close, I contracted with three additional counties for death investigation services starting January 1, 1998. I could see this was going to be more than I could handle alone, and I knew I had to make some changes.

Medical school teaches many things, but one thing it does not teach is business administration. Then, just when I needed him most, my good friend and mentor Dr. Bandt, who had successfully managed a busy hospital laboratory for years, stepped back into my life.

I had made the choice to leave the security of my hospital pathology group and start an independent forensic pathology practice. In early 1998, my father suggested I talk to Dr. Bandt about my new plans, since I had already plunged into my private forensic practice and was busy trying to keep up with all the new responsibilities. After leaving several messages on his home phone, I finally spoke with his wife, Ginny, who assured me he would call as soon as he returned from a trip overseas.

It was two weeks later, at 11:00 A.M. on a Thursday, when he called; I had just returned to my office from the morgue. "Of course I'll help you," he said, his voice bounding with enthusiasm. "I got home from Bosnia this morning. When do I start?"

"Any time you'd like!" I responded with a smile of relief on my face. "I just added three new counties, and I could really use your help and advice. Maybe you could stop by when the jet lag has worn off?"

A pause followed, and then he said, "Janis, three new counties in addition to the two you already have? That sounds a little like the boa constrictor that swallowed the pig! I'll see you Monday, then," and he hung up the phone.

THE SECOND TIME we worked together was different for both of us; Cal confessed he had never liked the administrative roles and was happy to get back to really practicing forensic medicine. I was relieved he was there to guide me and advise my early administrative efforts. I felt reassured by his wisdom, experience, and knowledge. I also began to realize how much I had learned about hospital pathology in the intervening years. I could feel his respect when I *knew* the diagnosis on a difficult case or microscope slide. I kidded him that if he were only twenty years younger, we could have practiced forensic pathology for a long time together. Most of all, though, we really had fun.

Usually, the only place he would sit was in *my* office, behind *my* desk, and on *my* chair. Occasionally I found him under the desk redesigning the wiring connections for my computer. One day, though, I returned from the autopsy suite to find him sitting at the secretary's desk, furiously typing. While she was at lunch, he had set up a complete toxicology accession system, used to track deaths due to various types of illicit drugs and medications. It is one that we use to this day.

Cal was a natural teacher with many areas of special interest, including neuropathology, the study of diseases and injuries to the central nervous system and the brain. This special interest earned him the nickname "Calvarium," which is the Latin term for the bones of the skull. He often lectured on and diagnosed many difficult and unusual disorders that affect the brain. Cal could also outline the basic chemistry of both obscure and common laboratory tests on a paper napkin at lunch, or talk for an hour on the maritime strategies of battles in the Pacific in World War II.

ONE SATURDAY AFTERNOON, the body of a forty-eight-year-old man was discovered collapsed on the floor of his rented home with debris and overturned furniture strewn around the room. His body showed no significant injuries, but the death scene and circumstances were suspicious. My investigator noted that a friend who had been interviewed mentioned the decedent had been experiencing increasingly severe headaches over the past two months.

Several law enforcement officers were in attendance when I began the postmortem early Sunday morning. Although the man's clothing was unkempt and soiled, I discovered no external injuries. Examination of the chest and abdominal organs showed no sign of disease. Then I began to examine the brain and found it remarkably swollen, much more so than I had ever seen before. Yet I saw no signs of bleeding or any evidence of a stroke.

Puzzled, I began to look more closely. I discovered a semi-translucent cyst, no bigger around than a dime, deep within an area known as the ventricular system, which handles the flow and drainage of the crystal-clear cerebral spinal fluid (CSF) that bathes the brain. Normally, the fluid gently flows from the deep central structures where it is formed through the central part of the brain and down to its base; it then circulates upward over the cerebral hemispheres before draining into the venous channels of the dura mater on the outside of the brain or flowing down around the spinal cord.

The cystic structure, which was unlike anything I had ever seen, seemed almost to float, making it mobile enough to obstruct the flow of CSF depending on the position of the head and the pull of gravity. If the flow of CSF was obstructed, pressure inside the head would quickly build in the brain. Both the officers looked to me for a definitive answer. "Is that it, Doc? Do we need to look any further at the scene?"

"Would you give me a moment?" I answered back.

Quickly I stripped off my gloves and excused myself from the autopsy suite. I snuck back to the little morgue office, closed the door, and paged Dr. Bandt. Within minutes the phone rang, and I grabbed it. "Dr. Bandt, thanks *so* much for calling me back!" I quickly explained the case, the concerns, and my findings and their unknown significance.

"Oh, sure, Janis, that sounds like a colloid cyst of the third ventricle. I saw one once about twenty years ago. The fellow had severe headaches which were positional. The cyst acted like a cork in a bottle, plugging and unplugging the outflow of cerebrospinal fluid. The buildup of pressure in the brain caused the headache."

"Oh, thank you so much. That's the diagnosis!" I exclaimed. "That is exactly what this man has, including the headaches. I'll release the scene and let the detectives go."

"I agree, Janis; tell them it is completely natural."

"Oh, one more thing," I said, noticing the unusual noise in the background. "Where are you, anyway?"

There was a pause. "In the airport in Denver; I'm flying on to visit my brother in Las Vegas this morning. When I received your page, we were just boarding. I made them hold the plane!"

"Oh my! Thank you so much for calling!" I laughed as we said good-bye. One of his daughters and her family lived in Colorado. And of course, that was just like Cal Bandt; he could make a diagnosis *anywhere* — he was always there for me!

SEVERAL YEARS PASSED, and my long-awaited forensic pathologist and now good friend, Dr. Butch Huston, joined my practice. Cal continued working, but now mainly came in periodically to review our problem cases, those not so easily diagnosed. I would ask him to come in to help me think; and that he did, dissecting and analyzing complex toxicology questions and medical problems with ease.

Then, during a routine physical examination, an X-ray caught a faint shadow on the edge of his left lung. When it failed to clear up with antibiotics, he had a biopsy performed, which indicated a possible tumor. I remember Cal calling me with the results; he reminded me he had smoked cigarettes many years ago. We were both keenly aware of the relationship of lung cancer to cigarette smoking.

Another biopsy was performed, and this time there was no doubt; my dear friend had lung cancer. Doctors recommended removal of the affected lobe of lung, a painful procedure Cal handled with courage. However, months later, additional tests revealed the spread of the cancer to a vertebra in the upper back. I remember the discouragement in his voice when he called to tell me. "We both know what this means, Janis," he said. I could hardly speak.

I think it was then that I learned the most from Cal Bandt. He resumed his life activities with deliberate vigor; he planned time to golf and fish with friends and took a trip to Mexico, spending three weeks there with all his family. Those months following his diagnosis, I noticed a subtle difference in our conversations. He seemed more direct when we discussed a case, urging me to search what I already knew till I arrived at the correct answer. He accompanied me and sat at my side during important meetings with law enforcement and county officials. I felt the invisible push as he taught me to trust myself, essentially showing me I could manage without him.

I realized this is what all great teachers do: they hold their students close and then gracefully let them go.

We never said good-bye. I got a note from him a week before his sudden but not unexpected death. He wrote that his golf game wasn't what it had been, but that he was happy. He said that life was good, that it had been a very good seventy years, and that he missed me. I made a mental note to visit him the following week.

Monday morning I was awakened by a phone call from his daughter informing me Cal had been brought to the hospital on Saturday evening with difficulty breathing and possible pneumonia. Apparently, he even looked at the results of his own lab tests and diagnosed his condition. Cal died suddenly on Sunday evening of respiratory failure. Ginny, his wife, asked me to speak at his funeral and I gladly agreed.

I realized Dr. Bandt had died in September on the eve of Yom Kippur, the time in the Jewish tradition when people review their lives and ask that their names be inscribed for one more year in the Book of Life. At first I thought how this was not to be; now I realize how incredibly meaningful the timing of his death really was.

For the visitation the night before the funeral, Cal's family created a wonderful tribute to his life. It was complete with photographs, books, his writings, memorabilia, beautiful music, and the Anoka County badge I had given him. Although I thought I knew a lot about him, I learned much more that evening, looking at photos of Cal golfing, riding horses, sailing on the lake near his home, and fishing. I hadn't realized how much he had loved being on (and in) the water.

I was unprepared for the depth and intensity of my grief when I left late that evening; I sat in the almost empty parking lot with tears streaming uncontrollably down my face and my head in my hands. Realizing I had a long way to drive home, I wiped my eyes, took a few deep breaths, and reached over to turn on the radio. I punched the button to the "oldies" station, knowing I could always count on some good rock and roll to lift my spirits.

Much to my amazement, from the radio came the words to the last verse of the very familiar Simon and Garfunkel song "Bridge over Troubled Water":

When you need a friend,
I'm sailing right behind.
Like a bridge over troubled water,
I will ease your mind.

A smile slowly replaced my tears. There it was, my own miracle. And the word *mind* wasn't lost on me either! "Thanks, Cal," I said to him and myself. "I'll count on that!"

EPILOGUE: GLIMPSES OF THE IMMORTAL MYSTERY

Death is not the opposite of Life. Life has no opposite.
Death is the opposite of Birth.

— ECKHART TOLLE, *STILLNESS SPEAKS*

When I testify in court, any speculation is always dismissed by the prosecutor or the defense attorney. "Stick to what you know, Doctor," they admonish me. "Remember the oath you swore here: 'To tell the truth, the whole truth, and nothing but the truth, so help me God.'"

Good advice, I think. How, then, to answer those who wonder if these recounted experiences are just "too good to be true" or who ask why they have not had a comforting dream or felt the presence of a loved one? There are no easy answers; however, I do know, from all the experiences that have been shared with me, that these messages are all around us, all the time. But often we don't notice. I also know that one has to be listening and looking, and when we begin to "awaken" everything changes. It has been said that the eye only sees what the mind knows. I would say, rather, that our senses recognize only what the heart remembers. These experiences cause us to remember — and to awaken.

That is when we begin to take the *next* step, and ask the *next* questions: "Who are we?" and "What really happens?" This is the stage that we seem to be approaching, collectively evolving toward, in part through interest in all things "forensic."

We see the truth about life and gain a deep knowing, a glimpse through the mysterious veil separating the living and the dead. I believe in my heart, I *know*, that life goes on... forever. Could this knowing be the essence of healing and hope? Is this the sacred observation that I chased and sought for all these years through my journey into medicine and forensic pathology?

I remember my own caveat about the investigation of a death: observe, don't judge. And Dr. Bandt's words, "Trust yourself; you'll know."

THESE ARE THE TRUTHS that I have rediscovered and hold dear.

Transitions are sacred times, but so, of course, is life sacred time. The high drama at the time of birth and death capture our attention, but more importantly allow glimpses into the great mysteries of life.

The extraordinary experiences that have been captured on these pages — and whispered thousands of times over hundreds of years — provoke a profound sense of well-being, of "feeling you're on solid ground." These gifts of a lifetime echo the wisdom of the ages. Their messages are not secrets or mysteries. The wisdom is as familiar as the smile of a dear friend, as heartwarming as the sunlight on a winter morning, as comforting as a good meal at the end of a busy day.

The wisdom is simply put, but not simple:

- There is a rhythm to life, and a season.

- Trust life, God, and trust the process, have faith.

- You are safe. All is well. Life will always go on. That means your life and the life of all others.

- You are deeply loved and never alone.

- You will see your loved ones again and again; and just the power of your thought will draw them near.

- You are more than you know, and you are more than your body. Care for all aspects of yourself. Care for all others as well. Be care-full. Be generous and humble. What you do for another, you do for yourself. Remember who you *really* are: one made in the image and likeness of God, woven from the immortal threads of Forever. Have no fear. Be well.

THESE BEAUTIFUL EXPERIENCES allow us to truly find ourselves again, to remember who we are, truly, and what we already know.

This "knowing beyond knowing" lets us heal our hearts, hope and dream, and dance and sway to the rhythm of life with compassion, kindness and courage, wonder and joy, the absence of fear… and the profound reassurance that all is well.

I have a deep feeling that the whole truth about the immortal mystery of Life is that everything truly *is* all right. And, of course, that changes everything.

ACKNOWLEDGMENTS

I am profoundly grateful to those who have shared their amazing and beautiful experiences with me; their voices ring with courage, clarity, and knowing. These extraordinary stories have inspired and comforted me and helped me remember my own truth.

My gratitude also extends to my family, friends, and co-workers, including:

My mother and father, Verda and Don, who read every word of countless manuscripts and offered comments and encouragement every step of the way.

Kathleen McMonigal, MD, my dear lifelong friend, who affirmed and encouraged my efforts to "see the patterns," and who applauded my efforts always, as only a good friend can do.

Marilyn Vermeer, my secretary and co-worker, who faithfully tracked, compiled, and updated all these stories. Her patience is surpassed only by her infinite kindness and goodwill.

Tom Baumgart, my dear husband and the love of my life, for his patience and understanding. And for assuming so many responsibilities while I devoted my time to this project.

Patricia Amatuzio, my "little" sister, who always finds the right word.

Gregg Mekler, for his powerful example of strength and insight.

David Brown, my wonderful friend, who reminds me always that laughter is the only cure for grief.

Duchie, my beautiful and beloved mastiff, who spent so many hours curled contentedly at my feet keeping me company while I wrote this book.

And to my family and friends both here and beyond: your names are written in my heart.

ABOUT THE AUTHOR

Janis Amatuzio, MD, trained at the University of Minnesota, the Hennepin County Medical Center, and the Medical Examiner's Office in Minneapolis before founding Midwest Forensic Pathology. P.A. Board–certified in anatomic, forensic, and clinical pathology, she is a recognized authority in forensic medicine and has developed many courses on topics such as death investigation, forensic nursing, and forensic medicine in mortuary science. Dr. Amatuzio serves as the medical examiner and a regional resource for multiple counties in Minnesota and Wisconsin. A dynamic speaker, she is frequently requested to speak on her experiences. Her previous book is *Forever Ours*.